Learning through Poetry

Consonant Blends and Digraphs

Mary Jo Fresch, Ph.D.
David L. Harrison, Litt.D

SHELL EDUCATION

Publishing Credits

Dona Herweck Rice, *Editor-in-Chief*; Robin Erickson, *Production Director*;
Lee Aucoin, *Creative Director*; Timothy J. Bradley, *Illustration Manager*;
Sara Johnson, M.S.Ed., *Editorial Director*; Jamey Acosta, *Senior Editor*;
Maribel Rendón, M.A.Ed., *Associate Education Editor*;
Evelyn Garcia, *Associate Education Editor*; Grace Alba, *Designer*;
Corinne Burton, M.A.Ed., *Publisher*

Image Credits

p. 34, mstay/istockphoto; p. 84 Janelle Bell-Martin; all other images Shutterstock

Standards

© 2004 Mid-continent Research for Education and Learning (McREL)
© 2007 Teachers of English to Speakers of Other Languages, Inc. (TESOL)
© 2007 Board of Regents of the University of Wisconsin System. World-Class Instructional Design and Assessment (WIDA). For more information on using the WIDA ELP Standards, please visit the WIDA website at www.wida.us.
© 2010 National Governors Association Center for Best Practices and Council of Chief State School Officers (CCSS)

Shell Education

5301 Oceanus Drive
Huntington Beach, CA 92649-1030
http://www.shelleducation.com
ISBN 978-1-4258-0974-4
© 2013 Shell Educational Publishing, Inc.

Table of Contents

Sound Beginnings

Rhythm and sounds are born with syllables. —Jean-Philippe Rameau

Becoming a reader is one of the greatest achievements of young learners. The complex process of reading begins long before children enter school or have any knowledge of print. Whether it's with a click of a lightbulb or with a slow and steady pace, most children develop the skills needed to become independent readers. It may be independently or under the guidance of a parent, teacher, or mentor, but young literacy learners eventually begin to connect the sounds of language with printed words on their journeys to becoming fluent readers.

Much can occur prior to the moment when children connect what they hear to what they see. Before children have the ability to understand that print represents particular sounds, they decipher the individual oral sounds of their language. Infants are born with the ability to hear all sounds from their mother tongue, filtering from all the possible sounds they are born to understand. Eventually, those sounds become part of the language they use to form words and sentences. This enables them to create meaning and communicate with others. For example, when children develop their understanding of the difference between "I can run" and "Can I run?," they first learn about the meanings of the words *I*, *can*, and *run*. By this time in their developmental process, they have learned which sounds make words and how to use those words to make meaning.

Children can also discover how much fun it is to experiment and play with language. Closely listening to children playing with language may provide us with a better understanding of how they come to understand the use of language. Gleeful shouts of "You're it!" during a game of tag, happy conversations about their favorite cartoon shows, caring comments to someone who fell off the slide, and playful rhymes for jumping rope all indicate that children are understanding the functions and the power of language.

Action Plan: Observing Children's Language Use

Halliday (1975) suggested that in the developmental process of meaning making, children learn to navigate seven specific functions of language in their quest to communicate effectively. These functions are instrumental (*I want*), regulatory (*Stop!*), personal (*I like*), interactional (*I'll help*), heuristic (*Why?*), imaginative (*I can fly!*), and informative (*That dog is big*). Observe a group of children playing. Listen to their conversation. What do you hear? Who seems to be utilizing all the functions? Think of ways to encourage play with these language functions, such as using the content or art activities that accompany the poems in this book.

Sound Beginnings *(cont.)*

Research continues to emphasize the importance of language development, especially in the years before formal schooling begins (Ehri et al. 2001). Specifically, hearing and playing with language will have important implications once reading instruction begins. Hart and Risley (2003) estimate that by age four, children of low socioeconomic status heard 30 million fewer words than their higher-income peers. When 29 children from the original study were longitudinally followed, Hart and Risley found that "children's rate of vocabulary growth and vocabulary use at age 3 was strongly associated with the grade 3 standardized scores in receptive vocabulary, listening, speaking, semantics, syntax, and reading comprehension" (Padak and Kindervater 2008, 58). Furthermore, Hart and Risley noted the importance of preschool experiences that would help close this gap and prepare children for kindergarten. Ehri and Roberts (2006) argue that "studies show that children who enter kindergarten with the ability to segment words into sounds and identify the names or sounds of letters make faster progress in learning to read in the first two years of instruction than children who lack these capabilities" (114). Therefore, teachers play a critical role in developing and supporting young children's language development (Wasik 2010).

It wasn't until the 1990s that researchers identified an important step in the meaning-making process—the development of phonemic awareness. The importance of the ability to hear the sounds of our language was best stated by Keith Stanovich (1993) when he observed that phonemic awareness is one of the best predictors of reading acquisition, even more so than IQ. Phonemic awareness is an important precursor to becoming a reader; it is a skill that can help children develop as language users as well as readers (Adams 1990). The National Institute of Child Health and Human Development (2000) concurred, stating that "correlational studies have identified phonemic awareness and letter knowledge as the two best school-entry predictors of how well children will learn to read during their first two years of school" (2–1). In a study conducted by Connie Juel (2006), her findings indicated that "children who struggled with learning to read words had entered the first grade with little phonemic awareness and were slow to acquire it. Poor readers had, as a group, less phonemic awareness at the *end* of the first grade than average and good readers had at the *beginning* of first grade" (410). Additionally, Juel, Griffith, and Gough (1986) found that students who performed at lower-performance levels in terms of phonemic awareness remained at the bottom through fourth grade. It is important that children recognize letter shapes and sounds in order to successfully transfer this connection-forming material when reading words (Ehri and Roberts 2006). The research cited above demonstrates that instruction and experience in phoneme manipulation are crucial for young learners. So if phonemic awareness is so important to literacy development, what exactly is it, and what connection does it have with phonological awareness?

Sound Beginnings (cont.)

What Is Phonemic Awareness?

Phonemic awareness is the ability to hear and manipulate the sounds (or phonemes) of language. A phoneme is the smallest unit of sound in our language (e.g., /b/, /s/, /ch/); all words are composed of phonemes. Since phonemes are units of sound, phonemic awareness does not require knowledge of print.

Understanding Phonemic Awareness

There are many skills related to phonemic awareness, and Marilyn Adams (1990) provided five levels necessary to maximize children's potential for later success in reading:

1. *Hearing rhymes and alliteration* (rhymes: *stop/hop/pop*; alliteration: *A peck of pickled peppers*)

2. *Doing oddity tasks* (What does not rhyme with the word *dog*? *log, shoe, fog, hog*)

3. *Blending and splitting syllables* (blending: /in/ /side/ = *inside*; splitting: *inside* = /in/ /side/)

4. *Performing phonemic segmentation* (*cat* = /c/ /a/ /t/)

5. *Performing phoneme manipulation tasks* (change the /b/ in the word *back* to /s/, which makes the word *sack*)

Providing practice for young learners to develop phonemic awareness is key to ensuring a successful start to their literacy journey. Juel (2006) notes that "We do have considerable longitudinal and experimental research to confirm that phonemic awareness is highly predictive to learning to read, that it can be promoted by instruction, and that this instruction seems to help children learn to read" (418). The National Institute of Child Health and Human Development (2000) also concluded that instruction in phonemic awareness advances children's ability to control phonemes in speech. That skill then transfers over to assisting children with comprehending what they read. Therefore, developing phonemic awareness provides a "strong and direct relationship to success and ease of reading acquisition" (Adams 1990, 82).

> **Action Plan: Demonstrating Phonemic Awareness**
>
> Have you ever heard children play with language by changing the sounds to make other words? For example, five-year-old Lauren demonstrated her phonemic awareness by calling her cat "Kitty Sitty Litty Ditty." Encourage this type of play by helping children manipulate the sounds of their own names.

Sound Beginnings (cont.)

How Do Phonemic Awareness and Phonological Awareness Differ?

Phonemic awareness is the beginning stage of phonological awareness (Armbruster, Lehr, and Osborn 2001). As aforementioned, phonemic awareness is the ability to hear and manipulate the separate phonemes of the language. Children can do this without understanding which letters or letter combinations represent the sound. Eventually, children will develop phonological awareness as they attempt to "map" the sounds they hear to the letters they see. Phonological awareness encompasses not only the manipulation of phonemes but also words, syllables, and onsets and rimes (2001). The development of phonemic awareness for beginning readers is important. Children who can hear the sounds of the language eventually move to reading the sounds of the language. Reading the sounds of the language puts them on the road to decoding and comprehending text.

Understanding Phonological Awareness

Lane and Pullen's (2004) synthesis of the research regarding phonological awareness pointed out several important generalizations:

- **A child's reading ability is directly related to his or her phonological awareness.** Findings indicate that children who have strong phonological awareness are often good readers because they can use the knowledge they have about letter-sound relationships to decode unfamiliar words. This is a useful skill in making children independent readers.

- **Phonological awareness is linked to proficiency in reading independently.** Having the ability to hear the sounds across a word appears to transfer to being able to take apart the sounds as we read across a word.

- **Phonological awareness precedes skilled decoding.** Therefore, opportunities to hear and play with the sounds of the language help students become aware of how sounds map onto print.

Sound Beginnings (cont.)

Traditionally, teaching children to match sounds to letters is called *phonics instruction*. Matching distinct sounds to the letters they see in print is the foundation of decoding. As awareness of print develops, the sounds and letters in a child's language begin to offer a young learner ways to read and gain meaning from text. While the term *phonics instruction* does not define a particular set of activities, children must understand the relationship of text and sound in order to become successful readers (Armbruster, Lehr, and Osborn 2001). Different educational resources may use different terms to describe the relationship between letters and sounds. Some common labels include *graphophemic, letter-sound associations, letter-sound correspondences, sound-symbol correspondences,* and *sound spellings.* These labels all mean the same thing: the teaching of the relationship between spoken sounds and written letters.

Instruction in these relationships can be very structured or embedded in other literacy work as children ask questions about new words they see in print. Either way, it helps children understand how written text connects to the sounds and words they hear in spoken language.

Action Plan: Observing Children's Development of Letter-Sound Relationships

Children's spelling attempts give us another view of their developing knowledge of letter-sound correspondences. A child who spells *cake* as *kak* is working across the sounds of the word and trying to make a one-to-one match between the sounds he or she hears and the letter or letters that often make that sound. As children continue to have experiences with print, they begin to develop memories of how a word looks, how certain letter combinations represent particular sounds, and how they can use what they hear to help them write. Linking writing to the activities suggested with the poems in this book is a good way to continue to nurture phonological awareness.

Playing with Sounds

Bringing children and poetry together can be one of the most exciting experiences in parenting or teaching.   —Lee Bennett Hopkins

There are many ways to help children develop knowledge in the sounds of their language. In this book, we present one of the ways: the use of poetry. But not just any poems will do! We provide entertaining and creative poems, specifically written to focus on the consonant blends and digraphs sound element. Hearing the poems several times allows every child to join in and learn in a fun and engaging manner.

What Experiences Should Teachers Provide?

Education is not the filling of a pail, but the lighting of a fire.   —William Butler Yeats

Playing with Phonemes

How do we know what experiences children should have? Instruction that supports learning while manipulating language can provide students with the opportunity to hear phonemes. A phoneme is the smallest unit of speech. It represents a single sound. Because our learners are young or new to the English language, having a fun romp through language is sure to entice every child. Knowing how to begin that romp is important. Louisa Moats (2000) suggests integrating auditory awareness by focusing on activities that entail the manipulation of speech sounds in words.

Action Plan: Learning while Manipulating Language

Rasinski and Padak (2008) suggest five types of phoneme manipulation to help young learners hear and play with language. If applied correctly, the following five types of manipulation can guide students toward learning the relationship between sounds and the letters that might represent them:

1. *Matching*: Which words sound the same at the beginning—*jump, dog, jar*?

2. *Isolation*: What is the first sound in the word *jump*?

3. *Blending*: What word is /d/ /o/ /g/?

4. *Substitution*: What word do I make if I change /d/ to /l/ in the word *dog*?

5. *Segmentation*: What sounds are in the word *game*?

Instruction that supports learning while manipulating language gives children experiences in hearing phonemes. Here, they understand that words can rhyme, have one or more syllables, can begin and end with the same sounds, and are made up of phonemes (Heilman 2002). Children begin to see these features in words through examining print. Practice in hearing and analyzing words is important to literacy development. Poetry allows us to tap into children's playfulness with language.

Why Poetry?

Griffith and Olson (1992) suggest that teachers should read rhyming texts to their students every day as a way to develop phonological awareness. Rhyming is one of the easier phonological tasks for children, and it appears to help them learn to decode text through analogy (Opitz 2000). For example, a student might think, "I know the word *hat* and I see the word *cat*—since they both end with the sound /at/, *cat* must sound like *hat*." Inkelas's (2003) longitudinal study found that playing with language develops knowledge not only of the sounds of the language but also of the meter and stress of poetry. Walton and Walton (2002) found that "prereading kindergartners can learn to begin reading by playing cooperative games that teach the rime analogy reading strategy and the implicated prereading skills of rhyming, initial phoneme identity, and letter-sound knowledge" (110).

Children are active constructors of language from the time they hear the first words spoken to them as infants all the way to their attempts to become readers and writers. Instruction that considers the needs of young language learners should be active, fun, and playful. That is where poetry comes in! No other form of English expression provides as many opportunities to read, hear, and practice phonemes. The manipulation of meter and sound are core characteristics of rhyming verse, and rhyming verse is easier to remember than any other linguistic construction.

Furthermore, children enjoy poetry. Learning something and enjoying it is a hard combination to beat. Much like a certain famous nanny's spoonful of sugar, poetry provides an exciting and entertaining way to help children develop phonological awareness. While children like poetry for a variety of reasons, one thing they particularly love is anything that taps into humor. Contemporary poems for children offer a rich menu of giggles, snorts, and slap-your-leg guffaws.

Action Plan: Discover Your Favorite Poem

One of the best ways to bring poetry into the classroom is to share a personal favorite. It can be as simple as a nursery rhyme ("Hickory Dickory Dock") or a poem that you learned in school and still remember. If you need ideas, many wonderful poets provide us with fun poetry. Besides the poems provided in this book, explore David L. Harrison's other poetry and other children's favorites, such as Shel Silverstein, Lee Bennett Hopkins, Douglas Florian, and Jack Prelutsky.

Why Poetry? *(cont.)*

Rasinski, Rupley, and Nichols (2008) remind us that "the use of rhyming poetry on a regular basis…can have a significant and positive impact on students' word recognition and reading fluency" (259). Additionally, teachers who read poems to their students demonstrate how intonation, expression, and timing play key roles in reading and understanding language. As Michael Opitz (2000) points out, "poetry can be used as a vehicle for helping children better understand the sound structure of their language. As they listen to poems, they develop a sense of how sounds are strung together to form words that convey intended meanings and images" (104). Finding good poems is key to engaging listeners. We must be selective, combing excellent literature for poems children will enjoy. Jim Trelease (1982) states, "Because good literature is precise, intelligent, colorful, sensitive, and rich in meaning, it offers the child his best hope of expressing what he feels" (19). Rhyming words, expressing feelings, and engaging in fun learning activities all help beginning readers feel successful. Why poetry? Poetry not only has the ability to engage and fascinate children, but it also offers creative outlets for self-expression and an excellent vehicle for teaching phonological awareness. Here we present specially written poems that allow children to explore the rhythm of poetry and connect print to the sounds of our language. Welcome! Let the fun begin!

Teaching the Lessons

To learn to read is to light a fire; every syllable that is spelled out is a spark. —Victor Hugo

The poems and activities in this book provide lessons for students who are moving from phonemic awareness to phonological awareness. For children still developing phonemic awareness, the lessons will encourage them to hear and play with sounds. For children ready for phonological activities, the lessons will encourage them to point out which letters and letter combinations make the sounds they hear in words. Additionally, the student activity sheets can allow children the opportunity to utilize their knowledge of sounds and print.

This book was designed with a foundation of integrating sound into the classroom. We hope you will find it helpful for students who are hearing and manipulating sounds to students ready to match sounds and print. Once you have selected a poem, you can decide which type of phoneme activity you want your students to engage in. There are five sound manipulation activities for every poem. These activities are a natural way to differentiate your instruction. You may have a small group of children who need additional practice with just sound matching. You may also create a small group of children ready to match sounds and print—phonics instruction. You can use the provided activity as well as the activity sheet to support these students. Your close observations of how the children participate in the sound manipulations will guide your decision to review the sound activities or expand their experiences into paper-and-pencil work.

As an optional way to enhance each individual poetry lesson, copy the poems for each student to keep as a personal, year-long collection in a pocket folder or a three-ring binder. Once you have completed the poem together, you may want to display it at learning centers, or on the bulletin board, to encourage the children to revisit it often.

The table on the following page provides an overview of the five sound manipulation activities that are provided with each poem in this book.

Teaching the Lessons (cont.)

Sound Manipulation Activities Overview

Phoneme (Sound) Matching

In a lesson of sound matching, the children listen for a specific beginning sound. For example, they might listen to "Fraidy Cat Frank" (page 49) and hear the /fr/ sound at the beginning of several words in the poem. You then ask the children which words from the poem do and do not begin with the /fr/ sound.

Phoneme (Sound) Isolation

Isolation lessons ask the children to listen for a specific sound within a given word. For example, when reading "Grandmas" (page 54) you can choose any word and ask, "What is the first sound in…*greasy*? What is the first sound in *growl*? In *grubs*?"

Phoneme (Sound) Blending

The next level of manipulation is blending. In this type of activity, we break a word into its separate phonemes and ask children to blend what they hear into the complete word. When saying words aloud to children, keep in mind that you want to slowly stretch the word to help them hear all the phonemes. For example, in "Croc and Cricket" (page 39), you could stretch out the word *crab* in two different ways: /k/ /r/ /a/ /b/ or /kr/ /ab/. You may also want to point to the word in the poem as you stretch it so that students who are reading can follow along with the print as you blend the sounds.

Phoneme (Sound) Substitution

Using a poem such as "Fly and Flea" (page 44), we ask children to listen to how the first letter(s), or onset, of the word is the same in words like *flea*, *flew*, and *flap*. Then, we ask them to change the onset to make new words not already in the poem. They might suggest *tea*, *blew*, or *cap*. These can be written on the board or chart paper to facilitate learning for children developing phonological awareness.

Sound Segmentation

In sound segmentation, ask children to do the opposite of what they did in blending. That is, ask them to take a word (*stop*) and tell us what sounds make up the word (/s/ /t/ /o/ /p/). You can do this by saying a word aloud for those children not yet reading print or by pointing to the word for your beginning readers. Ask children to stretch the sounds they hear. We often use the analogy of stretching a rubber band to help us slowly say the word.

#50974—*Learning through Poetry: Consonant Blends and Digraphs*

Teaching the Lessons *(cont.)*

This book presents 16 blends and digraphs poems. Each poem in this book focuses on consonant blends (where each consonant maintains its sound, but the two or three letters are blended together as in the letters *bl* or *fl*) or consonant digraphs (where two consonants create a new sound as in the letters *ch*, *sh*, or *th*).

A Closer Look at Blends and Digraphs

Consonant Blends or Digraphs	Sound
bl, br, cl, cr, fl, fr, gr, pl, sl, sn, sp, st,	each consonant maintains its own sound, but the two consonants are blended as we pronounce words.
th	second most frequently occurring digraph (/ng/ is the most frequently occuring digraph); Two sounds—voiced /th/, as in *this, than,* and *those,* and voiceless /th/, as in *thing, thaw,* and *month*
ch	third most frequently occurring digraph; Eighty-nine percent of the time sounds like /ch/ as in *church;* ten percent of the time sounds like /k/ as in *chaos* (words of Greek origin); one percent of the time sounds like /sh/ as in *che* (words of French origin)
sh	fourth most frequently occurring digraph; Consistent in sound of /sh/
wh	ninety percent of the time digraph sounds like /wh/ as in *wheel, where,* and *whiskers;* ten percent of the time digraph sounds like /w/ as in *what, why,* and *when;* the /wh/ phoneme is never at the end of a word

Teaching the Lessons (cont.)

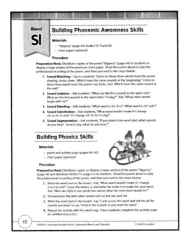

In the "Building Phonemic Awareness Skills" section, each sound manipulation activity suggests which words in the poem can be used for practice. Plan on spending about 10 minutes for each phonemic awareness activity and consider spreading the five manipulations over several days, reviewing the ones you already introduced.

Suggestions are made for those students ready to connect print and sound in the "Building Phonics Skills" section. These students can also be given the activity sheet to extend their experience working with consonant sounds in print.

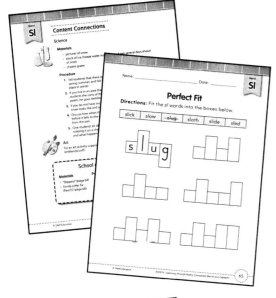

Cross-curricular connections expand the use of a single poem into multiple contexts. The "Content Connections" section of the lesson helps relate the poems to other educational areas such as mathematics, social studies, or science, while the art section (located on the Digital Resource CD) provides connections in dance, music, arts and crafts, drama, and movement.

The "School and Home Connection" contains a letter for children's families, explaining the lesson's poem and suggesting an activity for completion at home. A copy of the poem should be sent home along with the letter. Each poem is provided within the lesson, ready for you to photocopy and enlarge as you see fit.

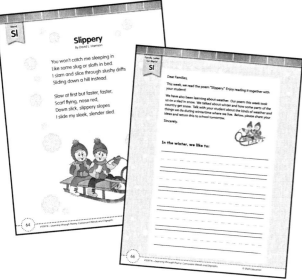

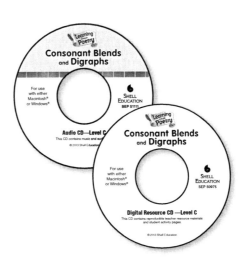

Peeking Into a Classroom

Mrs. Motz knew that young children love poetry, so *Learning through Poetry* was a natural choice for her. She loved the poems with specific elements of language highlighted through David Harrison's word choices. She also liked that she could extend the use of the poems across the curriculum. She could teach not only about language but also about content. The format of *Learning through Poetry* allowed her students to have multiple exposure to the words, rhyme, and content. Let's peek into Mrs. Motz's classroom to see how this worked. To begin, Mrs. Motz copied the poem "Choosy" (page 84) onto large chart paper and hung it on an easel. The children gathered on the floor in front of the easel.

Procedure: Day 1

Mrs. Motz read "Choosy" (page 84) aloud to the children. During this first time through, she read the poem solely for the fun of it, using lots of expression. She made certain the children could see the print on the chart paper and pointed to the words as she read aloud. After reading the poem, she invited the children to discuss it.

Mrs. Motz then read the poem aloud a second time. She asked the children to listen for rhyming words. During this reading, she paused to emphasize the words beginning with the consonant blend *ch*, pointing to each word as they discussed it (*chance, chili, cheap, chunky, cheese, chew, champion, choice, chicken, chop, chocolate, cherries*). Next, Mrs. Motz asked the children to listen to three words from the poem and identify which words began with the same initial sound: *chili, chop,* or *lose*. She then asked which words ended with the same sound: *chop, choose,* or *top*. She also pointed out the other words that rhyme: *true* and *chew, cheese* and *wheeze,* and *lose* and *choose*. Finally, Mrs. Motz read "Choosy" aloud again and asked the children to join in.

Procedure: Day 2

Mrs. Motz had reviewed the lesson completed the day before, identifying the rhyming words and the words beginning with the consonant blend *ch*. She then read the poem aloud, pointing to the words.

She asked the children to join in if they could, especially when they heard the words starting with consonant blend *ch*. She paused before saying the words beginning with the consonant blend *ch* to see if students remembered them. Mrs. Motz then asked the children to listen as she stretched the rhyming words from the poem. Could they tell her what word she was saying? For example, she said, "/ch/ /ew/," and the children responded, "chew." Mrs. Motz had the children practice blending several other words from the poem.

Peeking Into a Classroom *(cont.)*

Procedure: Day 3

Mrs. Motz read "Choosy" (page 84) aloud. She asked the children to listen as she stretched some of the *ch* words from the poem (/ch/ /ew/). She then asked them to blend the sounds together to "discover" the word. Mrs. Motz repeated this for several other words. Next, Mrs. Motz asked the children to think of additional words that start with the /ch/ sound. She wrote these on the board. Some words the children suggested were *choo-choo*, *change*, *Charlie*, and *chin*.

Mrs. Motz pointed out how the poem talks about cheese. She told the children that cheese is a dairy food. When we eat healthy, we might pick items from the dairy group. She then asked the children to think of ways they like to eat cheese. One child mentioned grilled cheese sandwiches that his Aunt Gigi makes him. Another child said his grandma makes good cheese pizza. The children continued to share, and Mrs. Motz recorded their ideas on the board.

Mrs. Motz made copies of the poem and family letter for the children to take home to share with their families. She encouraged them to discuss with their families about their favorite food with cheese in it or on it and write those ideas on the chart to bring back the next day.

Procedure: Day 4

Mrs. Motz recorded the family information on a large sheet of chart paper. She encouraged a discussion of what the children shared with their loved ones. Mrs. Motz then gave each child a large sheet of drawing paper. She also distributed scrap pieces of construction paper and told the children to tear shapes to make a picture of their favorite cheese food. When the children were done, their art pieces were displayed on a bulletin board titled "We Are Choosy About Our Cheese!"

Correlation to Standards

Purpose and Intent of Standards

Legislation mandates that all states adopt academic standards that identify the skills students will learn in kindergarten through grade 12. Many states also have standards for Pre-K. This same legislation sets requirements to ensure the standards are detailed and comprehensive.

Standards are designed to focus instruction and guide adoption of curricula. Standards are statements that describe the criteria necessary for students to meet specific academic goals. They define the knowledge, skills, and content students should acquire at each level. Standards are also used to develop standardized tests to evaluate students' academic progress. Teachers are required to demonstrate how their lessons meet state standards. State standards are used in the development of all of our products, so educators can be assured they meet the academic requirements of each state.

Shell Education is committed to producing educational materials that are research- and standards-based. In this effort, all products are correlated to the academic standards of the 50 states, the District of Columbia, and the Department of Defense Dependent Schools.

How to Find Standards Correlations

To print a customized correlation report of this product for your state, visit our website at **http://www.shelleducation.com** and follow the on-screen directions. If you require assistance in printing correlation reports, please contact Customer Service at 1-877-777-3450.

McREL Compendium

Shell Education uses the Mid-continent Research for Education and Learning (McREL) Compendium to create standards correlations. Each year, McREL analyzes state standards and revises the compendium. The McREL standards correlation can be found on the Digital Resourece CD (standards.pdf).

Common Core State Standards

The texts in this book are aligned to the Common Core State Standards (CCSS) for English Language Arts. The standards correlation can be found on pages 19–21 and on the Digital Resource CD (standards.pdf).

TESOL and WIDA Standards

The texts in this book promote English language development for English language learners. The standards correlation can be found on the Digital Resource CD (standards.pdf).

Common Core State Standards

The following chart helps organize the poems according to the Common Core State Standards.

Common Core State Standards		
Grade	**Phonological Awareness**	
	Standard	**Poem(s)**
Kindergarten	RF.K.2a—Recognize and produce rhyming words	All poems
	RF.K.2b—Count, pronounce, blend, and segment syllables in spoken words	All poems
	RF.K.2c—Blend and segment onsets and rimes of single-syllable spoken words	All poems
	RF.K.2d—Isolate and pronounce the initial, medial vowel, and final sounds (phonemes) in three-phoneme words	"Bratty" (page 29); "Clara" (page 34); "Fraidy Cat Frank" (page 49); "Plink" (page 59); "Slippery" (page 64); "Snack" (page 69); "Spunky Sparrow" (page 74); "Choosy" (page 84)
	RF.K.2e—Add or substitute individual sounds (phonemes) in simple, one-syllable words to make new words	All poems
	Phonics and Word Recognition	
	RF.K.3a—Demonstrate basic knowledge of one-to-one letter-sound correspondences by producing the primary or many of the most frequent sounds for each consonant	All poems
	RF.K.3b—Associate the long and short sounds with common spellings (graphemes) for the five major vowels	All poems
	RF.K.3c—Read common high-frequency words by sight	"Black and Blue" (page 24); "Bratty" (page 29); "Clara" (page 34); "Croc and Cricket" (page 39); "Fly and Flea" (page 44); "Fraidy Cat Frank" (page 49); "Grandmas" (page 54); "Plink" (page 59); "Slippery" (page 64); "Snack" (page 69); "Spunky Sparrow" (page 74); "When Kings Meet" (page 79); "Choosy" (page 84); "Shirley the Shark" (page 89); "Sister's Bad Thursday" (page 94); "Whoop It Up!" (page 99)
	RF.K.3d—Distinguish between similarly spelled words by identifying the sounds of the letters that differ	All poems

Common Core State Standards *(cont.)*

Common Core State Standards		
Grade	**Phonological Awareness**	
	Standard	**Poem(s)**
First Grade	RF.1.2a— Distinguish long from short vowel sounds in spoken single-syllable words	"Black and Blue" (page 24); "Bratty" (page 29); "Croc and Cricket" (page 39); "Fly and Flea" (page 44); "Fraidy Cat Frank" (page 49); "Grandmas" (page 54); "Plink" (page 59); "Slippery" (page 64); "Snack" (page 69); "Spunky Sparrow" (page 74); "When Kings Meet" (page 79); "Choosy" (page 84); "Shirley the Shark" (page 89); "Sister's Bad Thursday" (page 94)
	RF.1.2b—Orally produce single-syllable words by blending sounds (phonemes), including consonant blends	All poems
	RF.1.2c—Isolate and pronounce initial, medial vowel, and final sounds (phonemes) in spoken single-syllable words	"Bratty" (page 29); "Clara" (page 34); "Fraidy Cat Frank" (page 49); "Plink" (page 59); "Slippery" (page 64); "Snack" (page 69); "Spunky Sparrow" (page 74); "Choosy" (page 84)
	RF.1.2d—Segment spoken single-syllable words into their complete sequence of individual sounds (phonemes)	"Black and Blue" (page 24); "Bratty" (page 29); "Clara" (page 34); "Croc and Cricket" (page 39); "Fly and Flea" (page 44); "Fraidy Cat Frank" (page 49); "Grandmas" (page 54); "Plink" (page 59); "Slippery" (page 64); "Snack" (page 69); "Spunky Sparrow" (page 74); "When Kings Meet" (page 79); "Choosy" (page 84); "Shirley the Shark" (page 89); "Sister's Bad Thursday" (page 94); "Whoop It Up!" (page 99)

Common Core State Standards *(cont.)*

Common Core State Standards	
Grade	**Phonics and Word Recognition**
	Standard / **Poem(s)**

Grade	Standard	Poem(s)
First Grade	RF.1.3a—Know the spelling-sound correspondences for common consonant digraphs	"Black and Blue" (page 24); "Clara" (page 34); "Croc and Cricket" (page 39); "Fraidy Cat Frank" (page 49); "Grandmas" (page 54); "Plink" (page 59); "Slippery" (page 64); "Spunky Sparrow" (page 74); "When Kings Meet" (page 79); "Choosy" (page 84); "Shirley the Shark" (page 89); "Sister's Bad Thursday" (page 94)
	RF.1.3b—Decode regularly spelled one-syllable words	All poems
	RF.1.3c—Know final -e and common vowel team conventions for representing long vowel sounds	"Black and Blue" (page 24); "Bratty" (page 29); "Clara" (page 34); "Croc and Cricket" (page 39); "Fly and Flea" (page 44); "Fraidy Cat Frank" (page 49); "Grandmas" (page 54); "Plink" (page 59); "Slippery" (page 64); "Snack" (page 69); "Spunky Sparrow" (page 74); "When Kings Meet" (page 79); "Choosy" (page 84); "Shirley the Shark" (page 89); "Sister's Bad Thursday" (page 94); "Whoop It Up!" (page 99)
	RF.1.3d—Use knowledge that every syllable must have a vowel sound to determine the number of syllables in a printed word	All poems
	RF.1.3e—Decode two-syllable words following basic patterns by breaking the words into syllables	All poems
	RF.1.3f—Read words with inflectional endings	"Black and Blue" (page 24); "Bratty" (page 29); "Clara" (page 34); "Croc and Cricket" (page 39); "Fly and Flea" (page 44); "Fraidy Cat Frank" (page 49); "Plink" (page 59); "Slippery" (page 64); "Snack" (page 69); "When Kings Meet" (page 79); "Shirley the Shark" (page 89); "Sister's Bad Thursday" (page 94)
	RF.1.3g—Recognize and read grade-appropriate irregularly spelled words	"Black and Blue" (page 24); "Clara" (page 34); "Croc and Cricket" (page 39); "Grandmas" (page 54); "Slippery" (page 64); "Spunky Sparrow" (page 74)

Building Phonemic Awareness Skills

Materials

- "Black and Blue" (page 24; Audio CD: Track 01)
- chart paper (*optional*)

Procedure

Preparation Note: Distribute copies of the poem "Black and Blue" (page 24) to students or display a large version of the poem on chart paper. Read the poem aloud or play the professional recording of the poem, and then proceed to the steps below.

1. **Sound Matching**—Say to students, "Listen to these three words from the poem: *blue, day, blow*. Which have the same sound at the beginning? Listen to these three words from the poem: *blasted, Jay, lasted*. Which have the same sounds at the end?"

2. **Sound Isolation**—Ask students, "What are the first sounds in *blue*? "What are the first sounds in *bleak*? In *blew*?" Ask, "What other words begin with /bl/?"

3. **Sound Blending**—Ask students, "What word is /bl/ /ue/? What word is /bl/ /eak/?"

4. **Sound Substitution**—Ask students, "What word would I make if I change /bl/ to /d/ in *blue*? If I changed /bl/ to /b/ in *bleak*?"

5. **Sound Segmentation**—Ask students, "If you stretch the word *bleak*, what sounds do you hear? Stretch *blow*, what do you hear?"

Building Phonics Skills

Materials

- poem and activity page (pages 24–25)
- chart paper (*optional*)

Procedure

Preparation Note: Distribute copies or display a large version of the poem "Black and Blue" (page 24) and distribute *Bl or B?* (page 25) to students. Read the poem aloud or play the professional recording of the poem, and then proceed to the steps below.

1. Write the word *blue* on the board. Ask, "What word would I make if I change *bl* to *d* in *blue*?" Erase the letters *bl*, and write the letter *d* to make the new word. Ask, "Were we right in our prediction about what the new word would be?"

2. Demonstrate this with other words such as *blue/glue, bleak/beak, blew/dew*.

3. Write the word *bleak* on the board. Say, "Look across the word and tell me all the sounds you hear." Or say, "Stretch the sounds as you read the word."

4. Repeat the activity with the word *blow*. Have students complete the activity page for additional practice.

Content Connections

Science

Materials

- clipboard (one per student)
- field guide (found on the Digital Resource CD filename: fieldguide.pdf; one per student)
- crayons

Procedure

1. Before leaving the room, give each student a clipboard and a field guide.

2. Model for students how to use their crayons to color the color words.

3. Tell students to circle the color of any birds they see.

4. Read the second column to students and tell them that when they see a bird, they should put a tally mark under the picture of the wings if the bird is flying or a tally mark under the picture of the bird feet if the bird is walking.

5. Go outdoors with students, and sit (quietly) to watch for birds. If needed, help students mark their field guides. If possible, share the types of birds with students.

Art

For an art activity supporting this lesson, please see the Digital Resource CD (artblendbl.pdf).

School and Home Connection

Materials

- "Black and Blue" (page 24)
- *Family Letter for Blend Bl* (page 26)

Procedure

1. Attach the poem to the family letter.

2. When students return with their papers, ask them to tell what they saw when they birdwatched at home. Share any bird names their families wrote down.

3. Discuss what they learned. Did they see some of the same birds you saw in science?

#50974—Learning through Poetry: Consonant Blends and Digraphs

Black and Blue

By David L. Harrison

Blue Jay sat on a blackberry bush
Blaring to the sky,
"I'm so handsome!
I'm so pretty!
No bird's better than I!"

Blackbird blazed at Blue Jay, "Hey!
I have bleak news for you.
You can blow
And blah all day
But black is better than blue!"

"You blockhead!" blurted Blue Jay.
"You blowhard!" Blackbird blasted.
"I'm better!"
"I'm better!"
They blabbed and blew.
No telling how long it lasted.

Name: _____ Date: _____

Bl or B?

Directions: How should the word start? Write *bl* or *b*.

____ ____ _____ock	____ ____ _____ouse	____ ____ _____ird
____ ____ _____oat	____ ____ _____anket	____ ____ _____one

#50974—Learning through Poetry: Consonant Blends and Digraphs

Dear Families,

This week, we read the poem "Black and Blue." Enjoy reading it together with your student!

We have also been learning about birdwatching. Please go to a window or outdoors with your student and fill in the chart below. Return it to school tomorrow so we can share what you saw together.

Sincerely,

Color of Birds We Saw	What the Birds Were Doing	Names of Birds We Saw

Building Phonemic Awareness Skills

Materials

- "Bratty" (page 29; Audio CD: Track 02)
- chart paper (*optional*)

Procedure

Preparation Note: Distribute copies of the poem "Bratty" (page 29) to students or display a large version of the poem on chart paper. Read the poem aloud or play the professional recording of the poem, and then proceed to the steps below.

1. **Sound Matching**—Say to students, "Listen to these three words from the poem: *brother, broke, pain.* Which have the same sounds at the beginning? Listen to these three words from the poem: *brain, school, pain.* Which have the same sound at the end?"

2. **Sound Isolation**—Ask students, "What are the first sounds in *brain*? What are the first sounds in the word *brush*? In *Brother*?" Ask, "What other words begin with /br/?"

3. **Sound Blending**—Ask students, "What word is /br/ /ush/? What word is /br/ /ain/?"

4. **Sound Substitution**—Ask students, "What word would I make if I change /br/ to /r/ in *brain*? If I change /br/ to /r/ in *brush*?"

5. **Sound Segmentation**—Ask students, "If you stretch the word *Brad,* what sounds do you hear? Stretch *brown,* what do you hear?"

Building Phonics Skills

Materials

- poem and activity page (pages 29–30)
- chart paper (*optional*)

Procedure

Preparation Note: Distribute copies or display a large version of the poem "Bratty" (page 29) and distribute *Match the Picture* (page 30) to students. Read the poem aloud or play the professional recording of the poem, and then proceed to the steps below.

1. Write the word *brain* on the board. Ask, "What word would I make if I change *br* to *r* in *brain*?" Erase the letters *br,* and write the letter *r* to make the new word. Ask, "Were we right in our prediction about what the new word would be?"

2. Demonstrate this with other words such as *train*, *drain*, and *pain*.

3. Write the word *Brad* on the board. Say, "Look across the word and tell me all the sounds you hear." Or say, "Stretch the sounds as you read the word."

4. Repeat the activity with the word *brown*. Have students complete the activity page for additional practice.

Content Connections

Social Studies

Materials

- "Bratty" (page 29; Audio CD: Track 02)
- class rules (your own or ones you create together)
- chart paper

Procedure

1. Reread the poem and discuss how Brother "broke a rule."

2. What rules do you have in your classroom? Review the list you have or create one.

3. Take one of the rules and discuss how students must act to follow the rule.

4. Make a list on the board of the directions necessary to follow one of the rules.

Art

For an art activity supporting this lesson, please see the Digital Resource CD (artblendbr.pdf).

School and Home Connection

Materials

- "Bratty" (page 29)
- *Family Letter for Blend Br* (page 31)

Procedure

1. Attach the poem to the family letter.

2. When students return with their papers, ask them to share the steps to the rule they follow at home.

3. Discuss what they learned.

Bratty

By David L. Harrison

Brother brought
A brown mouse to school,
Which broke a rule
And that is not so cool.

Brad calls Brother
A brat with half a brain.
Brenda Jane
Calls Brother a brilliant pain.

Teacher called
To talk (again) to Mother.
Yet another
Bratty brush for Brother.

Name: _____ Date: _____

Match the Picture

Directions: Say the name of the picture. Draw a line from the picture to the letters of the beginning sound you hear.

br	b

Dear Families,

This week, we read the poem "Bratty." Enjoy reading it together with you student!

We have also been learning about how to follow a rule. Below, write a rule you have in your family. Then, write the steps your student must complete in order to follow the rule (for instance, if a rule is that all family members take their plates to the sink after eating, the steps might be: pick up the plate, carefully carry it to the counter, place the plate on the counter). Return this paper to school tomorrow.

Sincerely,

Rule:

_____

- -

_____

Steps:

_____

- -

_____
_____

- -

_____
_____

- -

_____

Blend

Cl

Building Phonemic Awareness Skills

Materials

- "Clara" (page 34; Audio CD: Track 03)
- chart paper (*optional*)

Procedure

Preparation Note: Distribute copies of the poem "Clara" (page 34) to students or display a large version of the poem on chart paper. Read the poem aloud or play the professional recording of the poem, and then proceed to the steps below.

1. **Sound Matching**—Say to students, "Listen to these three words from the poem: *Clara, closet, solo*. Which have the same sounds at the beginning? Listen to these three words from the poem: *done, clump, one*. Which have the same sound at the end?"

2. **Sound Isolation**—Ask students, "What are the first sounds in *clarinet*? What is the first sound in *clamor*. In *clump*?" Ask, "What other words begin with /cl/? (Be sure to have fun with the phrase "clicky-clacky-clinky.")

3. **Sound Blending**—Ask students, "What word is /cl/ /ump/? What word is /cl/ /aimed/?"

4. **Sound Substitution**—Ask students, "What word would I make if I change /cl/ to /l/ in *clump*? If I change /cl/ to /d/ in *clump*?"

5. **Sound Segmentation**—Ask students, "If you stretch the word *clapped*, what sounds do you hear? Stretch *class*, what do you hear?"

Building Phonics Skills

Materials

- poem and activity page (pages 34–35)
- chart paper (*optional*)

Procedure

Preparation Note: Distribute copies or display a large version of the poem "Clara" (page 34) and distribute *Complete the Words* (page 35) to students. Read the poem aloud or play the professional recording of the poem, and then proceed to the steps below.

1. Write the word *clump* on the board. Ask, "What word would I make if I change *cl* to *l* in *clump*?" Erase the letters *cl*, and write the letter *l* to make the new word. Ask "Were we right in our prediction about what the new word would be?"

2. Demonstrate this with other words such as *dump*, *bump*, and *hump*.

3. Write the word *clapped* on the board. Say, "Look across the word and tell me all the sounds you hear." Or say, "Stretch the sounds as you read the word."

4. Repeat the activity with the word *class*. Have students complete the activity page for additional practice.

Content Connections

Social Studies

Materials

- "Clara" (page 34; Audio CD: Track 03)

Procedure

1. Reread the poem.

2. Tell students that some of the other students in Clara's class didn't seem to like the music she played. Discuss how the students in Clara's class could have behaved when listening to her play another song.

3. Ask students to share a song they like. If they can, ask them to sing some of it, suggesting others join in if they can. Discuss the songs mentioned as a class.

4. Discuss how people can like different things, such as music or art, and that we should always be polite, even if we don't always agree.

Art

For an art activity supporting this lesson, please see the Digital Resource CD (artblendcl.pdf).

School and Home Connection

Materials

- "Clara" (page 34)
- *Family Letter for Blend Cl* (page 36)

Procedure

1. Attach the poem to the family letter.

2. When students return with their papers, ask them to share the songs their families like.

3. Discuss what they learned. Did some families suggest the same song?

Clara

By David L. Harrison

Clara got a clarinet for Christmas,
She screeched a tune for Show-and-Tell today,
We clenched our teeth and claimed we loved her music,
She clobbered the notes but squeaked and squawked away.

The keys clattered clicky-clacky-clinky
The class clapped when she was clearly done,
Clueless Clara thought we liked the clamor,
"Thanks!" she said. "I know another one!"

Now the class has climbed inside the closet,
We crawled and clawed beneath this clump of clothes.
We beg you don't let Clara ever find us!
She'll play another solo if she knows!

Complete the Words

Directions: Clara's clarinet plays *cl* words. Write four real *cl* words using the letters below.

ean	ea	ap	ay	ip	oe

cl _____

cl _____

cl _____

cl _____

Use one of the words you made in a sentence.

_____

_____

_____

_____

 #50974—Learning through Poetry: Consonant Blends and Digraphs

Dear Families,

This week, we read the poem "Clara." Enjoy reading it together with your student!

We have also been learning about the songs we like. Below, tell us a song your family likes. Help your student practice the song so he or she can sing it in school tomorrow. Please return this sheet to school tomorrow.

Sincerely,

Our family likes the song:

_____

_____

_____

_____

Building Phonemic Awareness Skills

Materials

- "Croc and Cricket" (page 39; Audio CD: Track 04)
- chart paper (*optional*)

Procedure

Preparation Note: Distribute copies of the poem "Croc and Cricket" (page 39) to students or display a large version of the poem on chart paper. Read the poem aloud or play the professional recording of the poem, and then proceed to the steps below.

1. **Sound Matching**—Say to students, "Listen to these three words from the poem: *cricket, cracker, sweet.* Which have the same sounds at the beginning? Listen to these three words from the poem: *love, lucky, dove.* Which have the same sound at the end?"

2. **Sound Isolation**—Ask students, "What are the first sounds in *crabs*? What are the first sounds in *critters*? In *crocodile*?" Ask, "What other words begin with /cr/?"

3. **Sound Blending**—Ask students, "What word is /cr/ /ow/? What word is /cr/ /ane/?"

4. **Sound Substitution**—Ask students, "What word would I make if I change /cr/ to /t/ in *crow*? If I change /cr/ to /l/ in *crane*?"

5. **Sound Segmentation**—Ask students, "If you stretch the word *crave*, what sounds do you hear? Stretch *crane*, what do you hear?"

Building Phonics Skills

Materials

- poem and activity page (pages 39–40)
- chart paper (*optional*)

Procedure

Preparation Note: Distribute copies or display a large version of the poem "Croc and Cricket" (page 39) and distribute *CRossword Fun* (page 40) to students. Read the poem aloud or play the professional recording of the poem, and then proceed to the steps below.

1. Write the word *crow* on the board. Ask, "What word would I make if I change *cr* to *t* in *crow*?" Erase the letters *cr*, and write the letter *t* to make the new word. Ask, "Were we right in our prediction about what the new word would be?"

2. Demonstrate this with other words such as *row*, *grow*, and *flow*.

3. Write the word *crave* on the board. Say, "Look across the word and tell me all the sounds you hear." Or say, "Stretch the sounds as you read the word."

4. Repeat the activity with the word *crane*. Have students complete the activity page for additional practice.

#50974—*Learning through Poetry: Consonant Blends and Digraphs*

Content Connections

Math

Materials

- 3' sheet of paper with an outline of a crocodile
- 1.5" sheet of paper with an outline of a cricket
- board to display pictures

Procedure

1. Post the pictures of the crocodile and cricket side by side on a bulletin board or other display board.

2. Ask students, "Which is bigger?" Ask, "What other animals are as big or bigger than the crocodile?" Record students' responses.

3. Ask students, "What other animals are as small as or smaller than the cricket?" Record students' responses. Look around the classroom and ask students other comparison questions.

Art

For an art activity supporting this lesson, please see the Digital Resource CD (artblendcr.pdf).

School and Home Connection

Materials

- "Croc and Cricket" (page 39)
- *Family Letter for Blend Cr* (page 41)

Procedure

1. Attach the poem to the family letter.

2. When students return with their papers, ask them to share their big and little comparisons.

3. Discuss what they learned.

Croc and Cricket

By David L. Harrison

A crocodile and a cricket
Fell in love.
He crooned, "I'm crazy about you,
Wuvvy-dove."

The cricket cried, "I'm lucky
That we met!
I wuv you more than cracker
Crumbs, my pet."

"I wuv you more than crabs,"
Her lover cooed.
She said, "My darling, eating
Critters is rude."

"But snooky-wookums," he said,
"I crave my meat!"
She whispered, "Honey-bunny,
You're so sweet."

He croaked, "No crow or crane
To crunch and crack?"
"Not even," she said, "a crispy
Crawfish snack."

To give the croc credit,
He didn't fight
But he did insist on ice cream
Every night.

Name: _____ Date: _____

CRossword Fun

Directions: Circle the *cr* words in the box below.

croc   crazy   cricket   cream   crow   crane

c	r	i	c	k	e	t
e	c	r	a	z	y	r
c	r	o	c	y	o	w
w	c	r	e	a	m	e
h	c	r	o	w	a	m
c	s	c	r	a	n	e

Use one of the words you found in a sentence.

_____

- -

_____

_____

- -

_____

#50974—*Learning through Poetry: Consonant Blends and Digraphs*   © Shell Education

Dear Families,

This week, we read the poem "Croc and Cricket." Enjoy reading it together with your student!

We have also been learning about comparing sizes—big and small. Look around your home and help your student find several items you can compare in size. For example, a table is big, and a spoon is small. Fill in the chart below and return it to school tomorrow.

Sincerely,

In our home, we found these things we could compare:

Big	Little

#50974—*Learning through Poetry: Consonant Blends and Digraphs*

Blend

Fl

Building Phonemic Awareness Skills

Materials

- "Fly and Flea" (page 44; Audio CD: Track 05)
- chart paper (*optional*)

Procedure

Preparation Note: Distribute copies of the poem "Fly and Flea" (page 44) to students or display a large version of the poem on chart paper. Read the poem aloud or play the professional recording of the poem, and then proceed to the steps below.

1. **Sound Matching**—Say to students, "Listen to these three words from the poem: *fly, said, flea*. Which have the same sounds at the beginning? Listen to these three words from the poem: *fly, stew, try*. Which have the same sound at the end?"

2. **Sound Isolation**—Ask students, "What are the first sounds in the word *fly*? What are the first sounds in the word *flea*? In *flap*?" Ask, "What other words begin with /fl/?"

3. **Sound Blending**—Ask students, "What word is /fl/ /ea/? What word is /fl/ /ap/?"

4. **Sound Substitution**—Ask students, "What word would I make if I change /fl/ to /n/ in *flap*? If I change /fl/ to /t/ in *flea*?"

5. **Sound Segmentation**—Ask students, "If you stretch the word *flea*, what sounds do you hear? Stretch *fly*, what do you hear?"

Building Phonics Skills

Materials

- poem and activity page (pages 44–45)
- chart paper (*optional*)

Procedure

Preparation Note: Distribute copies or display a large version of the poem "Fly and Flea" (page 44) and distribute *Making Fl Words* (page 45) to students. Read the poem aloud or play the professional recording of the poem, and then proceed to the steps below.

1. Write the word *flap* on the board. Ask, "What word would I make if I change *fl* to *n* in *flap*?" Erase the letters *fl*, and write the letter *n* to make the new word. Ask, "Were we right in our prediction about what the new word would be?"

2. Demonstrate this with other words such as *cap*, *rap*, and *tap*.

3. Write the word *flea* on the board. Say, "Look across the word and tell me all the sounds you hear." Or say, "Stretch the sounds as you read the word."

4. Repeat the activity with the word *fly*. Have students complete the activity page for additional practice.

#50974—*Learning through Poetry: Consonant Blends and Digraphs* © Shell Education

Content Connections

Science

Materials

- "Fly and Flea" (page 44; Audio CD: Track 05)
- chart with the following three headings: *Insects That Fly*, *Animals That Fly*, *Things People Make That Fly*

Procedure

1. Reread the poem and discuss with students which words show that Fly and Flea were flying (e.g., flew, flutter, flap).

2. Show the chart with the three headings to students. Tell students to think of anything that flies. Where should it go on the chart? Record students' responses.

3. Use two of the words students added to the chart in place of Fly and Flea in the poem (e.g., Grasshopper and Bee flew down the flue and flipped in a pot of stew).

4. Ask students which two words from the chart were their favorites in place of Fly and Flea.

Art

For an art activity supporting this lesson, please see the Digital Resource CD (artblendfl.pdf).

School and Home Connection

Materials

- "Fly and Flea" (page 44)
- *Family Letter for Blend Fl* (page 46)

Procedure

1. Attach the poem to the family letter.
2. When students return with their papers, ask them to share their drawings.
3. Discuss what they learned.

Fly and Flea

By David L. Harrison

Fly
And Flea
Flew down
The flue
And flipped in a pot of stew.

"Help!"
Cried Fly.
"We'll drown!"
Cried Flea.
"What are we going to do?"

"Don't flutter!"
Said Fly.
"Don't flap!"
Said Flea.
"Float on our backs or we'll die!"

"Yum!"
Said Flea
To Fly,
"This stew
Has a flavor you really must try."

"Wow!"
Said Fly.
"Now,"
Said Flea,
"This gives me a clever plan."

"Eat!"
Said Flea.
"I am!"
Said Fly.
And together they emptied the pan.

#50974—Learning through Poetry: Consonant Blends and Digraphs

Name: _____ Date: _____

Making Fl Words

Directions: Fly and Flea fell in some stew. Use the correct letters below to make real *fl* words in the stew pot.

ea	ew	y	r	is
ag	ip	iff	at	am

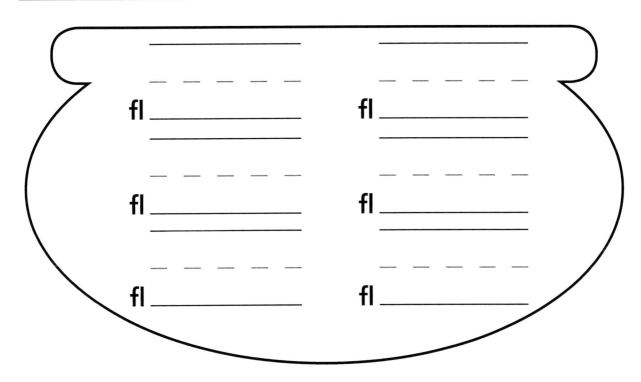

fl _____   fl _____

fl _____   fl _____

fl _____   fl _____

Use one of your words in a sentence.

_____

_____

_____

_____

Dear Families,

This week, we read the poem "Fly and Flea." Enjoy reading it together with your student!

We have also been learning about flight. We talked about insects, birds, and things people make that can fly. Talk with your student about what he or she learned at school about things that can fly. Then, ask your student what his or her favorite insect, animal, or object is that can fly. In the space below, have your student draw (and color, if you wish) his or her favorite thing that can fly. Return the picture to school tomorrow.

Sincerely,

My favorite thing that can fly is:

Building Phonemic Awareness Skills

Materials

- "Fraidy Cat Frank" (page 49; Audio CD: Track 06)
- chart paper (*optional*)

Procedure

Preparation Note: Distribute copies of the poem "Fraidy Cat Frank" (page 49) to students or display a large version of the poem on chart paper. Read the poem aloud or play the professional recording of the poem, and then proceed to the steps below.

1. **Sound Matching**: Say to students, "Listen to these three words from the poem: *frog, Frank, say*. Which have the same sounds at the beginning? Listen to these three words from the poem: *fret, stop, get*. Which have the same sound at the end?"

2. **Sound Isolation:** Ask students, "What are the first sounds in *fret*? What are the first sounds in the word *frog*? In *frisky*?" Ask, "What other words begin with /fr/?"

3. **Sound Blending:** Ask students, "What word is /fr/ /og/? What word is /fr/ /eak/?"

4. **Sound Substitution:** Ask students, "What word would I make if I change /fr/ to /d/ in *frog*? If I change /fr/ to /l/ in *freak*?"

5. **Sound Segmentation:** Ask students, "If you stretch the word *fret*, what sounds do you hear? Stretch *frog*, what do you hear?"

Building Phonics Skills

Materials

- poem and activity page (pages 49–50)
- chart paper (*optional*)

Procedure

Preparation Note: Distribute copies or display a large version of the poem "Fraidy Cat Frank" (page 49) and distribute *Matching F Words* (page 50) to students. Read the poem aloud or play the professional recording of the poem, and then proceed to the steps below.

1. Write the word *frog* on the board. Ask students, "What word would I make if I change *fr* to *d* in *frog*?" Erase the letters *fr*, and write the letter *d* to make the new word. Ask, "Were we right in our prediction about what the new word would be?"

2. Demonstrate this with other words such as *log, fog,* and *hog*.

3. Write the word *fret* on the board. Say, "Look across the word and tell me all the sounds you hear." Or say, "Stretch the sounds as you read the word."

4. Repeat the activity with the word *frog*. Have students complete the activity page for additional practice.

Content Connections

Science

Materials

- pictures of the three stages of a frog's life
- paper
- marker

Procedure

1. Show the pictures of the frog's life cycle to students. Ask them which picture is the frog. Then, tell them that the other two pictures are part of the frog's life cycle.

2. Ask students to help you put the pictures in the correct order. What in the picture can help them decide in what order the pictures should be placed?

3. Tell students the name of each stage (*egg, tadpole, frog*), write them on a sheet of paper, and then write each name by the correct picture.

4. Ask students if they can think of anything else that begins as an egg, has a second or third stage, and then becomes fully grown (e.g., egg, chick, hen; egg, caterpillar, pupa, butterfly).

Art

For an art activity supporting this lesson, please see the Digital Resource CD (artblendfr.pdf).

School and Home Connection

Materials

- "Fraidy Cat Frank" (page 49)
- *Family Letter for Blend Fr* (page 51)

Procedure

1. Attach the poem to the family letter.

2. When students return with their papers, ask them to share the life cycle their families discussed. Record students' responses on the chart and discuss what they learned.

Fraidy Cat Frank

By David L. Harrison

My friend Frank
Is afraid of frogs.
They make Frank frown,
They make Frank fret.

Frank can't say
Why they freak him out
And make him frantic
As he can get.

But a frolicking frog
Frightens Frank,
And a frisky frog
Is free to hop

'Til fraidy cat Frank,
In a frantic frenzy,
Yells and begs
Those frogs to stop!

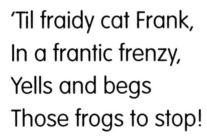

#50974—Learning through Poetry: Consonant Blends and Digraphs

Name: _____ Date: _____

Matching F Words

Directions: Which pictures start with *fr* and which start with *f*? Draw a line to show how each word sounds at the beginning.

fr	f

Dear Families,

This week, we read the poem "Fraidy Cat Frank." Enjoy reading it together with your student!

We have also been learning about the life cycle of a frog. Our frog started as an egg, became a tadpole, and finally a frog! Help your student think of something else that begins as an egg, then has a "next stage," and then becomes an adult. Please send this to share at school tomorrow.

Sincerely,

The life cycle we talked about was:

_____

_____

_____

_____

_____

_____

_____

#50974—Learning through Poetry: Consonant Blends and Digraphs

Blend

Gr

Building Phonemic Awareness Skills

Materials

- "Grandmas" (page 54; Audio CD: Track 07)
- chart paper (*optional*)

Procedure

Preparation Note: Distribute copies of the poem "Grandmas" (page 54) to students or display a large version of the poem on chart paper. Read the poem aloud or play the professional recording of the poem, and then proceed to the steps below.

1. **Sound Matching**—Say to students, "Listen to these three words from the poem: *gruff, grin, roll.* Which have the same sounds at the beginning? Listen to these three words from the poem: *grits, pits, gross.* Which have the same sound at the end?"

2. **Sound Isolation**—Ask students, "What are the first sounds in the word *grizzlies*? What are the first sounds in the word *growl*? In *grasshopper*?" Ask, "What other words begin with /gr/?"

3. **Sound Blending**—Ask students, "What word is /gr/ /oan/? What word is /gr/ /uff/?"

4. **Sound Substitution**—Ask students, "What word would I make if I change /gr/ to /l/ in *groan*? If I change /gr/ to /p/ in *grin*?"

5. **Sound Segmentation**—Ask students, "If you stretch the word *groan*, what sounds do you hear? Stretch *grunt*, what do you hear?"

Building Phonics Skills

Materials

- poem and activity page (pages 54–55)
- chart paper (*optional*)

Procedure

Preparation Note: Distribute copies or display a large version of the poem "Grandmas" (page 54) and distribute *GReat Words* (page 55) to students. Read the poem aloud or play the professional recording of the poem, and then proceed to the steps below.

1. Write the word *grin* on the board. Ask, "What word would I make if I change *gr* to *p* in *grin*?" Erase the letters *gr*, and write the letter *p*. Ask, "Were we right in our prediction about what the new word would be?"

2. Demonstrate this with other words such as *fin*, *tin*, and *spin*.

3. Write the word *groan* on the board. Say, "Look across the word and tell me all the sounds you hear." Or say, "Stretch the sounds as you read the word."

4. Repeat the activity with the word *grunt*. Have students complete the activity page for additional practice.

Content Connections

Math

Materials

- instant oatmeal packets (one packet per 2–3 students)
- large mixing bowl
- hot water (boiled or microwaved)
- bowls and spoons (one each per student)

Procedure

1. Tell students that Grandma Grizzly made gruel (a thin, cooked cereal).

2. In the large mixing bowl, pour the number of packets needed so each student will have a taste of oatmeal. (**Note:** Some students may have gluten intolerance, so you may want to use instant rice cereal for them.) As you pour the contents of each packet in the bowl, tell students you are adding "more" and count the number of packets.

3. Measure the amount of water you need for the number of packets you have and heat it. Discuss the amount of water you are using and how the recipe on the packet tells how much to add. Stir the water into the oats and serve to each student.

Art

For an art activity supporting this lesson, please see the Digital Resource CD (artblendgr.pdf).

School and Home Connection

Materials

- "Grandmas" (page 54)
- *Family Letter for Blend Gr* (page 56)

Procedure

1. Attach the poem to the family letter.

2. When students return with their papers, ask them to share the recipe their family sent.

3. You could photocopy the recipes in a booklet to send home to the families. The cover can be a blank sheet of paper that students can decorate.

Grandmas

By David L. Harrison

Gruff old grandpa grizzlies growl
Grimly when they eat.
With grabby claws
They fill their paws
With veggies, fruit, and meat.

Grandma grizzlies' "grrrs" are sweet,
They love to spoil their cubs
With grasshopper grits,
Cherry pits,
And gruel with greasy grubs.

We think gruel with grubs is gross
But grand-cub grizzlies slurp it,
They grin and groan,
Grunt and moan,
And roll their eyes and burp it.

GReat Words

Directions: Cut out and glue the correct letters on the boxes below to make six words that start with *gr*.

gr ☐   gr ☐

gr ☐   gr ☐

gr ☐   gr ☐

Write one of your words in a sentence.

_____

_____

_____

_____

_____

_____

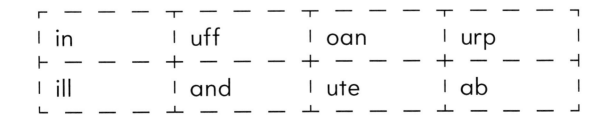

| in | uff | oan | urp |
| ill | and | ute | ab |

#50974—Learning through Poetry: Consonant Blends and Digraphs

Dear Families,

This week, we read the poem "Grandmas." Enjoy reading it together with your student!

We have also been learning about cooking. We made oatmeal and talked about measuring for a recipe. Talk with your student about something your family likes to cook together or a favorite recipe. Please share the recipe below and return it to school.

Sincerely,

Recipe for:

_____

- -

_____

How to make:

_____

- -

_____

_____

- -

_____

_____

- -

_____

Building Phonemic Awareness Skills

Materials

- "Plink" (page 59; Audio CD: Track 08)
- chart paper (*optional*)

Procedure

Preparation Note: Distribute copies of the poem "Plink" (page 59) to students or display a large version of the poem on chart paper. Read the poem aloud or play the professional recording of the poem, and then proceed to the steps below.

1. **Sound Matching**—Say to students, "Listen to these three words from the poem: *plan, plate, quick*. Which have the same sounds at the beginning? Listen to these three words from the poem: *plate, plan, mate*. Which have the same sound at the end?"

2. **Sound Isolation**—Ask students, "What are the first sounds in the word *plump*? What are the first sounds in the word *plum*? In *plan*?" Ask, "What other words begin with /pl/?"

3. **Sound Blending**—Ask students, "What word is /pl/ /an/? What word is /pl/ /ate/?"

4. **Sound Substitution**—Ask students, "What word would I make if I change /pl/ to /r/ in *plan*? If I change /pl/ to /p/ in *plan*?"

5. **Sound Segmentation**—Ask students, "If you stretch the word *plump*, what sounds do you hear? Stretch *plopped*. What do you hear?"

Building Phonics Skills

Materials

- poem and activity page (pages 59–60)
- chart paper (*optional*)

Procedure

Preparation Note: Distribute copies or display a large version of the poem "Plink" (page 59) and distribute *Pl Crossword* (page 60) to students. Read the poem aloud or play the professional recording of the poem, and then proceed to the steps below.

1. Write the word *plan* on the board. Ask, "What word would I make if I change *pl* to *r* in *plan*?" Erase the letters *pl*, and write the letter *r* to make the new word. Ask, "Were we right in our prediction about what the new word would be?"

2. Demonstrate this with other words such as *tan*, *can*, and *man*.

3. Write the word *plump* on the board. Say, "Look across the word and tell me all the sounds you hear." Or say, "Stretch the sounds as you read the word."

4. Repeat the activity with the word *plopped*. Have students complete the activity page for additional practice.

#50974—*Learning through Poetry: Consonant Blends and Digraphs*

Content Connections

Science

Materials

- "Plink" (page 59; Audio CD: Track 08)
- plastic tubs that will hold several inches of water
- water
- plastic toy bug
- objects that will float (e.g., cork, ice cubes, styrofoam, feather)
- objects that will sink (e.g., golf ball, crayon, coins)

Procedure

1. Reread the poem, placing the plastic bug inside the tub of water. The bug was worried he would "sink." Discuss what *sink* means.

2. Discuss what happened next in the poem (an ice cube was dropped in the glass so the bug could crawl up on it). Drop an ice cube in the water so that students understand that the cube floats.

3. Show students the containers of water and the objects they are to "test" for sinking and floating. Allow time for students to experiment with the objects.

4. At the end of the exploration time, ask students to tell you which objects floated and which objects sank. Separate these objects into two piles.

Art

For an art activity supporting this lesson, please see the Digital Resource CD (artblendpl.pdf).

School and Home Connection

Materials

- "Plink" (page 59)
- *Family Letter for Blend Pl* (page 61)

Procedure

1. Attach the poem to the family letter.

2. When students return with their papers, ask them to share the "float and sink" objects their families experimented with.

3. Discuss what they learned.

Plink

By David L. Harrison

A bug plopped in my drink,
Ker-plink!
A rather pleasant bug,
I think,
Plainly plump and plum-
Pink.
"Help!" she pleaded, "I may
Sink!

"Please hurry! I'm getting
Sick!
Throw me a rope, a plank,
A stick!"
I plotted a plan and plotted it
Quick,
I plopped an ice cube in,
Ker-plick.

Lucky for her, I wasn't
Late,
That cube saved her from an awful
Fate,
Then I gently spooned her on my
Plate,
And off she flew singing,
"Thank you, mate!"

#50974—Learning through Poetry: Consonant Blends and Digraphs

Name: _____ Date: _____

Pl Crossword

Directions: Read the clues below. Use these words to finish the crossword.

plate	plan	play	plum	plug

Down

1. I like to _____ soccer.

2. Please _____ in the lamp.

3. I have a _____ to save the bug!

Across

2. I eat the food on my _____.

3. _____ is a color and a fruit.

Dear Families,

This week, we read the poem "Plink." Enjoy reading it together with your student!

We have also been learning about objects that float or sink. Fill a container or your sink with water. Find a few objects that you can test to see if they float or sink (for instance, a rubber band, paper clip, fork, straw). Record below what you and your student found out about each object and return this paper to school tomorrow.

Sincerely,

Object We Tested	Did it float or sink?

#50974—*Learning through Poetry: Consonant Blends and Digraphs*

Blend **Sl**

Building Phonemic Awareness Skills

Materials

- "Slippery" (page 64; Audio CD: Track 09)
- chart paper (*optional*)

Procedure

Preparation Note: Distribute copies of the poem "Slippery" (page 64) to students or display a large version of the poem on chart paper. Read the poem aloud or play the professional recording of the poem, and then proceed to the steps below.

1. **Sound Matching**—Say to students, "Listen to these three words from the poem: *sleeping, slushy, down.* Which have the same sounds at the beginning? Listen to these three words from the poem: *red, faster, sled.* Which have the same sound at the end?"

2. **Sound Isolation**—Ask students, "What are the first sounds in the word *slick*? What are the first sounds in the word *slam*? In *slug*?" Ask, "What other words begin with /sl/?"

3. **Sound Blending**—Ask students, "What word is /sl/ /ice/? What word is /sl/ /ed/?"

4. **Sound Substitution**—Ask students, "What word would I make if I change /sl/ to /b/ in *sled*? If I change /sl/ to /b/ in *slug*?"

5. **Sound Segmentation**—Ask students, "If you stretch the word *sled*, what sounds do you hear? Stretch *slug*, what do you hear?"

Building Phonics Skills

Materials

- poem and activity page (pages 64–65)
- chart paper (*optional*)

Procedure

Preparation Note: Distribute copies or display a large version of the poem "Slippery" (page 64) and distribute *Perfect Fit* (page 65) to students. Read the poem aloud or play the professional recording of the poem, and then proceed to the steps below.

1. Write the word *sled* on the board. Ask, "What word would I make if I change *sl* to *b* in *sled*?" Erase the letters *sl*, and write the letter *b* to make the new word. Ask, "Were we right in our prediction about what the new word would be?"

2. Demonstrate this with other words such as *fed, led,* and *red*.

3. Write the word *sled* on the board. Say, "Look across the word and tell me all the sounds you hear." Or say, "Stretch the sounds as you read the word."

4. Repeat the activity with the word *slug*. Have students complete the activity page for additional practice.

Content Connections

Science

Materials

- pictures of snow
- block of ice (freeze water inside a bread pan several days ahead of time)
- cheese grater

Procedure

1. Tell students that there are four seasons in a year. They are winter, spring, summer, and fall (autumn). Explain that this poem takes place in winter.

2. If you live in an area that has snow in the winter, discuss with students the sorts of things you can do outside in the snow (in the poem, he goes sledding).

3. If you do not have snow where you live, have some pictures of what snow looks like and activities you can do in the snow.

4. Discuss how when the sky gets cold enough, moisture (rain) is frozen before it falls to the ground and becomes snow. Remove the ice from the pan.

5. Give students an idea of how snow feels by taking the ice and rubbing it on a cheese grater over their hands. Discuss how it feels and what happens as they hold it.

Art

For an art activity supporting this lesson, please see the Digital Resource CD (artblendsl.pdf).

School and Home Connection

Materials

- "Slippery" (page 64)
- *Family Letter for Blend Sl* (page 66)

Procedure

1. Attach the poem to the family letter.

2. When students return with their papers, ask them to share their snow activity ideas.

3. Discuss what they learned.

Slippery
By David L. Harrison

You won't catch me sleeping in
Like some slug or sloth in bed.
I slam and slice through slushy drifts
Sliding down a hill instead.

Slow at first but faster, faster,
Scarf flying, nose red,
Down slick, slippery slopes
I slide my sleek, slender sled.

#50974—Learning through Poetry: Consonant Blends and Digraphs   © Shell Education

Name: _____ Date: _____

Perfect Fit

Directions: Fit the *sl* words into the boxes below.

slick	slow	~~slug~~	sloth	slide	sled

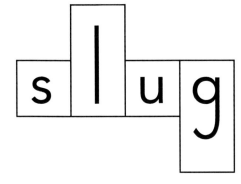

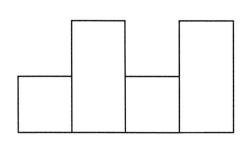

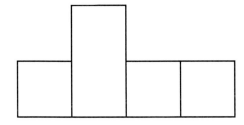

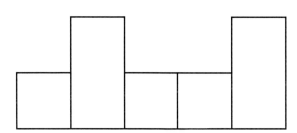

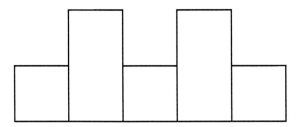

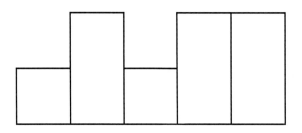

#50974—*Learning through Poetry: Consonant Blends and Digraphs*

Dear Families,

This week, we read the poem "Slippery." Enjoy reading it together with your student!

We have also been learning about weather. Our poem this week took us on a sled in snow. We talked about winter and how some parts of the country get snow. Talk with your student about the kinds of weather and things we do during wintertime where we live. Below, please share your ideas and return this to school tomorrow.

Sincerely,

In the winter, we like to:

_____

_____

_____

_____

_____

_____

_____

_____

_____

Building Phonemic Awareness Skills

Materials

- "Snack" (page 69; Audio CD: Track 10)
- chart paper (*optional*)

Procedure

Preparation Note: Distribute copies of the poem "Snack" (page 69) to students or display a large version of the poem on chart paper. Read the poem aloud or play the professional recording of the poem, and then proceed to the steps below.

1. **Sound Matching**—Say to students, "Listen to these three words from the poem: *snail, pardon, snake*. Which have the same sounds at the beginning? Listen to these three words from the poem: *snicker, sniffed, quicker*. Which have the same sound at the end?"

2. **Sound Isolation**—Ask students, "What are the first sounds in the word *sneeze*? What are the first sounds in the word *sneak*? In *snake*?" Ask, "What other words begin with /sn/?"

3. **Sound Blending**—Ask students, "What word is /sn/ /ake/? What word is /sn/ /eeze/?"

4. **Sound Substitution**—Ask students, "What word would I make if I change /sn/ to /b/ in *snake*? If I change /sn/ to /p/ in *snail*?"

5. **Sound Segmentation**—Ask students, "If you stretch the word *snap*, what sounds do you hear? Stretch *snail*, what do you hear?"

Building Phonics Skills

Materials

- poem and activity page (pages 69–70)
- chart paper (*optional*)

Procedure

Preparation Note: Distribute copies or display a large version of the poem "Snack" (page 69) and distribute *Sorting Sn Words* (page 70) to students. Read the poem aloud or play the professional recording of the poem, and then proceed to the steps below.

1. Write the word *snake* on the board. Ask, "What word would I make if I change *sn* to *b* in *snake*?" Erase the letters *sn*, and write the letter *b* to make the new word. Ask, "Were we right in our prediction about what the new word would be?"

2. Demonstrate this with other words such as *take*, *rake*, and *cake*.

3. Write the word *snap* on the board. Say, "Look across the word and tell me all the sounds you hear." Or say, "Stretch the sounds as you read the word."

4. Repeat the activity with the word *snail*. Have students complete the activity page for additional practice.

#50974—Learning through Poetry: Consonant Blends and Digraphs

Content Connections

Math

Materials

- 1" paper snail and 20" paper snake (outlines found on Digital Resource CD filename: snailandsnake.pdf)
- rulers (1 per every 2 students)
- yardstick

Procedure

1. Display the snail and the snake.

2. Using a yardstick, show how you can measure each. For the snail, use a one-foot ruler. Discuss how the snake is longer (or bigger) than the snail.

3. Show students where the numbers are on a ruler. Have a few classroom items you can measure together (e.g., chart paper, book, crayon).

4. Distribute a ruler to each pair of students and ask them to move around the classroom, measuring items of their choice.

5. Allow time for exploration, and then come together to discuss the items they measured. Ask them to share some of the measurements they took.

Art

For an art activity supporting this lesson, please see the Digital Resource CD (artblendsn.pdf).

School and Home Connection

Materials

- "Snack" (page 69)
- *Family Letter for Blend Sn* (page 71)

Procedure

1. Attach the poem to the family letter.

2. When students return with their papers, ask them to share one item they measured at home and how big it was.

3. Discuss what they learned.

Snack

By David L. Harrison

Said a snooty, snippy,
Snobbish snail
To a sniffly snake
In the garden,
"Don't sneeze on me,
You snotty snake!"

The snake sniffed,
"Beg your pardon?
Snapdragons always
Make me sneeze.
You're rude
To sneer and snicker."

The snide snail tried
To sneak away
But SNAP!
The snake
Was quicker.

#50974—Learning through Poetry: Consonant Blends and Digraphs

Name: _____ Date: _____

Sorting Sn Words

Directions: The snake and snail need more *sn* words! Cut out and sort the pictures of the *sn* and words that don't start with *sn*. Glue them in the correct column.

Sn	Not Sn

#50974—Learning through Poetry: Consonant Blends and Digraphs   © Shell Education

Dear Families,

This week, we read the poem "Snack." Enjoy reading it together with your student!

We have also been learning about measurement. We used rulers and measured items in our classroom. Below is a 6 inch ruler. Please cut it out (or use your own ruler if you have one), and then help your student measure some items in your home. Please fill out the chart below and return it to school tomorrow for sharing.

Sincerely,

Item Measured	How Big It Was

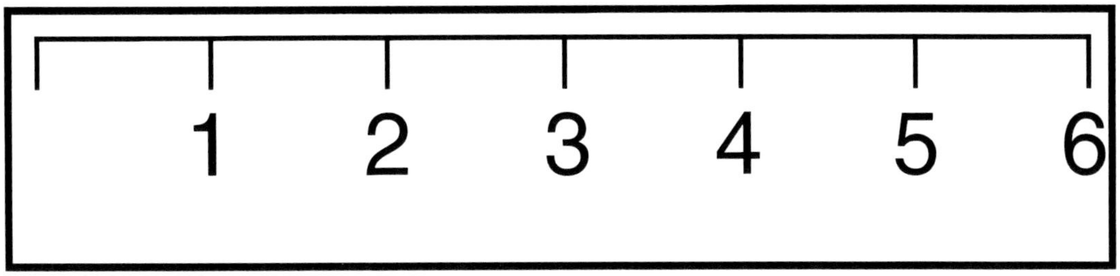

1 2 3 4 5 6

#50974—*Learning through Poetry: Consonant Blends and Digraphs*

Blend

Sp

Building Phonemic Awareness Skills

Materials

- "Spunky Sparrow" (page 74; Audio CD: Track 11)
- chart paper (*optional*)

Procedure

Preparation Note: Distribute copies of the poem "Spunky Sparrow" (page 74) to students or display a large version of the poem on chart paper. Read the poem aloud or play the professional recording of the poem, and then proceed to the steps below.

1. **Sound Matching**—Say to students, "Listen to these three words from the poem: *spice, chew, sputter.* Which have the same sounds at the beginning? Listen to these three words from the poem: *speak, matter, beak.* Which have the same sound at the end?"

2. **Sound Isolation**—Ask students, "What are the first sounds in the word *sparrow*? What are the first sounds in the word *sputter*? In *speak*?" Ask, "What other words begin with /sp/?"

3. **Sound Blending**—Ask students, "What word is /sp/ /eak/? What word is /sp/ /ice/?"

4. **Sound Substitution**—Ask students, "What word would I make if I change /sp/ to /b/ in *speak*? If I change /sp/ to /n/ in *spice*?"

5. **Sound Segmentation**—Ask students, "If you stretch the word *speak*, what sounds do you hear? Stretch *spew*, what do you hear?"

Building Phonics Skills

Materials

- poem and activity page (pages 74–75)
- chart paper (*optional*)

Procedure

Preparation Note: Distribute copies or display a large version of the poem "Spunky Sparrow" (page 74) and distribute *Sp Words* (page 75) to students. Read the poem aloud or play the professional recording of the poem, and then proceed to the steps below.

1. Write the word *spice* on the board. Ask, "What word would I make if I change *sp* to *n* in *spice*?" Erase the letters *sp*, and write the letter *n* to make the new word. Ask, "Were we right in our prediction about what the new word would be?"

2. Demonstrate this with other words such as *rice, dice,* and *mice.*

3. Write the word *speak* on the board. Say, "Look across the word and tell me all the sounds you hear." Or say, "Stretch the sounds as you read the word."

4. Repeat the activity with the word *spew.* Have students complete the activity page for additional practice.

Content Connections

Social Studies

Materials

- "Spunky Sparrow" (page 74; Audio CD: Track 11)
- world map
- pictures of food (see procedure)

Procedure

1. Reread the poem. Make a list on the board of all the food in the poem (spaghetti, butter, jam, ham, spareribs).

2. Ask students which of these foods they have tried. Explain that we can get all these foods in America, but some of the foods are originally from other countries.

3. Show the world map and point to each of the countries listed below, pinning a picture of the food associated with it near the country.

   Examples:

   - Italy—pizza
   - China—rice
   - Mexico—tacos or empanadas
   - Greece—feta cheese
   - France—croissant
   - India—naan

4. Ask students if they know any other foods from other cultures. Add these to the map.

Art

For an art activity supporting this lesson, please see the Digital Resource CD (artblendsp.pdf).

School and Home Connection

Materials

- "Spunky Sparrow" (page 74)
- *Family Letter for Blend Sp* (page 76)

Procedure

1. Attach the poem to the family letter.

2. When students return with their papers, ask them to share what they discussed with their families.

3. Discuss what they learned about each other.

#50974—*Learning through Poetry: Consonant Blends and Digraphs*

Spunky Sparrow

By David L. Harrison

My brother says,
If you sprinkle spice
On a sparrow's beak,
You can teach it to speak.

My sister says,
You can feed it spaghetti
Or butter and jam
But leave off the ham.

My brother says,
It will love spareribs
But ham it can't chew
And will sputter and spew.

I think they're teasing.
No matter how spunky,
A sparrow can't speak
With ham in its beak.

Name: _____ Date: _____

Sp Words

Directions: Help Sparrow put *sp* words around his tree! Use the correct letters below to make real *sp* words.

ice	eak	ag	ot	ept	in	ill	ort	ave

sp _____

sp _____

sp _____

sp _____

sp _____

sp _____

Use a word you made in a sentence.

_____

_____

_____

© Shell Education   #50974—*Learning through Poetry: Consonant Blends and Digraphs*

Dear Families,

This week, we read the poem "Spunky Sparrow." Enjoy reading it together with your student!

We have also been learning about foods from around the world. We talked about the American foods in the poem and some food from other countries. Talk with your student about your family background and what food is special to you (for instance, food from Japan or Grandma's best macaroni and cheese). Share with us by filling in your special food below. Please return it to school tomorrow.

Sincerely,

Our family's food that is special to our background is:

_____

_____

_____

_____

_____

_____

Building Phonemic Awareness Skills

Materials

- "When Kings Meet" (page 79; Audio CD: Track 12)
- chart paper (*optional*)

Procedure

Preparation Note: Distribute copies of the poem "When Kings Meet" (page 79) to students or display a large version of the poem on chart paper. Read the poem aloud or play the professional recording of the poem, and then proceed to the steps below.

1. **Sound Matching**—Say to students, "Listen to these three words from the poem: *sturdy, chill, stars.* Which have the same sounds at the beginning? Listen to these three words from the poem: *chill, stream, hill.* Which have the same sound at the end?"

2. **Sound Isolation**—Ask students, "What are the first sounds in the word *stars*? What are the first sounds in the word *steer*? In *stallion*?" Ask, "What other words begin with /st/?"

3. **Sound Blending**—Ask students, "What word is /st/ /amps/? What word is /st/ /ars/?"

4. **Sound Substitution**—Ask students, "What word would I make if I change /st/ to /l/ in *stamps*? If I change /st/ to /b/ in *stands*?"

5. **Sound Segmentation**—Ask students, "If you stretch the word *stars*, what sounds do you hear? Stretch *steel*, what do you hear?"

Building Phonics Skills

Materials

- poem and activity page (pages 79–80)
- chart paper (*optional*)

Procedure

Preparation Note: Distribute copies or display a large version of the poem "When Kings Meet" (page 79) and distribute *Circling St Words* (page 80) to students. Read the poem aloud or play the professional recording of the poem, and then proceed to the steps below.

1. Write the word *stamps* on the board. Ask, "What word would I make if I change *st* to *l* in *stamps*?" Erase the letters *st*, and write the letter *l*. Ask, "Were we right in our prediction about what the new word would be?"

2. Demonstrate this with other words such as *camps, ramps, stands,* and *bands.*

3. Write the word *stars* on the board. Say, "Look across the word and tell me all the sounds you hear." Or say, "Stretch the sounds as you read the word."

4. Repeat the activity with the word *steel.* Have students complete the activity page for additional practice.

#50974—Learning through Poetry: Consonant Blends and Digraphs

Content Connections

Social Studies

Materials

- "When Kings Meet" (page 79; Audio CD: Track 12)
- chart paper
- clock with movable hands (*optional*)

Procedure

1. Reread the poem. Explain how the horse and steer met at night. Ask students to share other things that we do at night. Record students' responses on the board.

2. Discuss with students the meaning of *night*. Discuss the meaning of *sunset* (check the local news for your sunset time).

3. If you have a clock with movable hands, show the current time and move the hands ahead to sunset time.

4. Discuss with students how at sunset time, we often are finishing dinner or getting ready for bed. Talk about other activities families do at night.

Art

For an art activity supporting this lesson, please see the Digital Resource CD (artblendst.pdf).

School and Home Connection

Materials

- "When Kings Meet" (page 79)
- *Family Letter for Blend St* (page 81)

Procedure

1. Attach the poem to the family letter.

2. When students return with their papers, ask them to tell you about a family routine. If you like, record these on the board or chart paper.

3. Discuss what they learned.

When Kings Meet
By David L. Harrison

The champion stallion
stalks through the night,
stamps the cold earth
with hooves strong as steel.

On a nearby hill,
breath steaming
in the evening chill,
a sturdy steer
stands stiff-legged,
staring without a sound.

Their eyes meet, stern, steady,
as the two great champions stand
like statues beneath the stars,
then walk together like two kings
down to the stream to drink.

#50974—Learning through Poetry: Consonant Blends and Digraphs

Name: _____ Date: _____

Circling St Words

Directions: Circle the pictures of the *st* words.

#50974—*Learning through Poetry: Consonant Blends and Digraphs*   © *Shell Education*

Dear Families,

This week, we read the poem "When Kings Meet." Enjoy reading it together with your student!

We have also been learning about our nighttime routines (the horse and the steer in the poem met at night to go to the stream together). We discussed activities our families do at night. We talked about how many of these activities happen after sunset.

Talk with your student about a routine your family has in the evening. Tell us about it below and return this paper to school tomorrow for sharing.

Sincerely,

In the evening, our family...

_____

- -

_____
_____

- -

_____
_____

- -

_____
_____

- -

_____

#50974—*Learning through Poetry: Consonant Blends and Digraphs*

Digraph Ch

Building Phonemic Awareness Skills

Materials

- "Choosy" (page 84; Audio CD: Track 13)
- chart paper (*optional*)

Procedure

Preparation Note: Distribute copies of the poem "Choosy" (page 84) to students or display a large version of the poem on chart paper. Read the poem aloud or play the professional recording of the poem, and then proceed to the steps below.

1. **Sound Matching**—Say to students, "Listen to these three words from the poem: *chili, chop, lose.* Which have the same sounds at the beginning? Which other words in the poem begin with *ch*? Listen to these three words from the poem: *chop, choose, top.* Which have the same sound at the end?"

2. **Sound Isolation**—Ask students, "What are the first sounds in the word *chance*? What are the first sounds in the word *chew*? In *chicken*?" Ask, "What other words begin with /ch/?"

3. **Sound Blending**—Ask students, "What word is /ch/ /op/? What word is /ch/ /eap/?"

4. **Sound Substitution**—Ask students, "What word would I make if I change /ch/ to /p/ in *chop*? If I change /ch/ to /l/ in *cheap*?"

5. **Sound Segmentation**—Ask students, "If you stretch the word *chew*, what sounds do you hear? Stretch *chop*, what do you hear?"

Building Phonics Skills

Materials

- poem and activity page (pages 84–85)
- chart paper (*optional*)

Procedure

Preparation Note: Distribute copies or display a large version of the poem "Choosy" (page 84) and distribute *Is It Ch or C?* (page 85) to students. Read the poem aloud or play the professional recording of the poem, and then proceed to the steps below.

1. Write the word *chop* on the board. Ask, "What word would I make if I change *ch* to *p* in *chop*?" Erase the letters *ch*, and write the letter *p*. Ask, "Were we right in our prediction about what the new word would be?"

2. Demonstrate this with other words such as *cop* (this provides an opportunity to point out how *ch* and *c* are different and how *ch* works), *drop*, and *stop*.

3. Write the word *chop* on the board. Say, "Look across the word and tell me all the sounds you hear." Or say, "Stretch the sounds as you read the word."

4. Repeat the activity with the word *chew*. Have students complete the activity page for additional practice.

#50974—Learning through Poetry: Consonant Blends and Digraphs © Shell Education

Content Connections

Science

Materials

- "Choosy" (page 84; Audio CD: Track 13)
- chart paper

Procedure

1. Reread the poem.

2. Tell students that when we eat healthy, we might choose a dairy food, and cheese belongs to the dairy group.

3. Ask students to share their favorite way to eat cheese (if a student has a dairy allergy, you might have him or her help you call on students so he or she can still participate).

4. Record students' suggestions (e.g., grilled cheese, pizza, on top of spaghetti, crackers and cheese).

Art

For an art activity supporting this lesson, please see the Digital Resource CD (artdigraphch.pdf).

School and Home Connection

Materials

- "Choosy" (page 84)
- *Family Letter for Digraph Ch* (page 86)

Procedure

1. Attach the poem to the family letter.

2. When students return with the paper, record the family suggestions of good foods with cheese.

3. Discuss what they learned.

Choosy

By David L. Harrison

Don't take a chance on chili
With cheap, chunky cheese,
I tell you true,
Once you chew,
You'll get a champion wheeze.

Buy choice cheese for chili
Or chicken or a chop,
And you'll never lose
For dessert when you choose
Chocolate with cherries on top.

#50974—Learning through Poetry: Consonant Blends and Digraphs

Name: _____ Date: _____

Is It Ch or C?

Directions: Look at each picture. How does the word start? Circle *ch* or *c*.

ch   c   ch   c   ch   c

ch   c   ch   c   ch   c

#50974—*Learning through Poetry: Consonant Blends and Digraphs*

Dear Families,

This week, we read the poem "Choosy." Enjoy reading it together with your student!

We have also been learning about cheese and different ways to eat it. Talk with your student about your family's favorite food with cheese. Tell us about your favorite below and return this paper to school tomorrow. If your student has a dairy allergy, share what he or she likes to eat in place of cheese.

Sincerely,

Our favorite food with cheese is:

Building Phonemic Awareness Skills

Materials

- "Shirley the Shark" (page 89; Audio CD: Track 14)
- chart paper (*optional*)

Procedure

Preparation Note: Distribute copies of the poem "Shirley the Shark" (page 89) to students or display a large version of the poem on chart paper. Read the poem aloud or play the professional recording of the poem, and then proceed to the steps below. Suggestion: Emphasize the incorrect words while reading the poem.

1. **Sound Matching**—Say, "Listen to these three words from the poem: *Shirley, shark, sleeping.* Which have the same sounds at the beginning? Listen to these three words from the poem: *sheep, shark, asleep.* Which have the same sound at the end?"

2. **Sound Isolation**—Ask students, "What are the first sounds in the word *sheep*? What are the first sounds in the word *shark*? In *Shirley*?" Ask, "What other words begin with /sh/?"

3. **Sound Blending**—Ask students, "What word is /sh/ /ark/? What word is /sh/ /eep/?"

4. **Sound Substitution**—Ask students, "What word would I make if I change /sh/ to /d/ in *shark*? If I change /sh/ to /d/ in *sheep*?"

5. **Sound Segmentation**—Ask students, "If you stretch the word *shark*, what sounds do you hear? Stretch *sheep*, what do you hear?"

Building Phonics Skills

Materials

- poem and activity page (pages 89–90)
- chart paper (*optional*)

Procedure

Preparation Note: Distribute copies or display a large version of the poem "Shirley the Shark" (page 89) and distribute *Time to Sort!* (page 90) to students. Read the poem aloud or play the professional recording of the poem, and then proceed to the steps below.

1. Write the word *shark* on the board. Ask, "What word would I make if I change *sh* to *d* in *shark*?" Erase the letters *sh*, and write the letter *d*. Ask, "Were we right in our prediction about what the new word would be?"

2. Demonstrate this with other words such as *lark*, *park*, and *spark*.

3. Write the word *shark* on the board. Say, "Look across the word and tell me all the sounds you hear." Or say, "Stretch the sounds as you read the word."

4. Repeat the activity with the word *sheep*. Have students complete the activity page for additional practice.

#50974—Learning through Poetry: Consonant Blends and Digraphs

Content Connections

Social Studies

Materials

- blue bulletin board paper with wavy lines drawn on it (representing water)
- tan or brown bulletin board paper added to the bottom of the blue paper (representing sand)
- pictures of a beach (optional)
- pictures of the ocean (optional)

Procedure

1. Lay the paper on the floor to create an "ocean."

2. Ask students if anyone has ever been to the ocean. Discuss what you would see there (if your students have not had the opportunity to visit the ocean, provide pictures of a beach and the ocean).

3. Discuss what students might take with them to play at the beach. What food might they pack?

4. As a class, plan a trip to the ocean! If you don't live near the ocean, imagine such a trip.

Art

For an art activity supporting this lesson, please see the Digital Resource CD (artdigraphsh.pdf).

School and Home Connection

Materials

- "Shirley the Shark" (page 89)
- *Family Letter for Digraph Sh* (page 91)

Procedure

1. Attach the poem to the family letter.

2. When students return with their papers, ask them to share what their families wrote.

3. Discuss what they learned.

Shirley the Shark

By David L. Harrison

Shirley was a shand shark,
Oops, I meant a sand sark,
Sirley was a shand sark,
At last I got it right!

Anyway she saw a sip,
I meant to shay a shailing ship,
Wait—I meant a sailing sip,
At noon one stormy night.

On that ship she shaw shome sheep,
The seep she saw were fast asleep,
Shirley shaw some sheep asleep
Snoozing in the sun.

The captain's name was Sailor Sam,
When Shailor Sham shaw Shirley Shark,
He shouted, "Save the sleeping seep!
She'll swallow every one!"

Sho Shailor Sham shaved the sheep
Schmoozing in the shun that night
And Shirley Shand Shark shwam away
And shank in the shea out of shight.

#50974—Learning through Poetry: Consonant Blends and Digraphs

Name: _____ Date: _____

Time to Sort!

Directions: Cut out the word parts below. Put the word parts in the column where they belong to create a word. Some word parts can go in both!

Sh	S

ark	and	eep	ip
ank	un	irt	aw

#50974—*Learning through Poetry: Consonant Blends and Digraphs*

Dear Families,

This week, we read the poem "Shirley the Shark." Enjoy reading it together with your student!

We have also been learning about taking a trip to the ocean. We talked about what we would take with us. Below, please share your ideas of what your family would take if you could travel to the ocean for a day. Return this to school tomorrow so that we can share your ideas!

Sincerely,

If our family could travel the ocean for a day, we would take:

_____

_____

_____

_____

_____

_____

_____

Digraph Th

Building Phonemic Awareness Skills

Materials

- "Sister's Bad Thursday" (page 94; Audio CD: Track 15)
- chart paper (*optional*)

Procedure

Preparation Note: Distribute copies of the poem "Sister's Bad Thursday" (page 94) to students or display a large version of the poem on chart paper. Read the poem aloud or play the professional recording of the poem, and then proceed to the steps below.

1. **Sound Matching**—Say to students, "Listen to these three words from the poem: *thumb, fussed, thump.* Which have the same sounds at the beginning? Listen to these three words from the poem: *moan, there, groan.* Which have the same sound at the end?"

2. **Sound Isolation**—Ask students, "What are the first sounds in the word *thud*? What are the first sounds in the word *thumb*? In *Thursday*?" Ask, "What other words begin with /th/?"

3. **Sound Blending**—Ask students, "What word is /th/ /ump/? What word is /th/ /ud/?"

4. **Sound Substitution**—Ask students, "What word would I make if I change /th/ to /b/ in *thump*? If I change /th/ to /m/ in *thud*?"

5. **Sound Segmentation**—Ask students, "If you stretch the word *thud*, what sounds do you hear? Now stretch *thump*, what do you hear?"

Building Phonics Skills

Materials

- poem and activity page (pages 94–95)
- chart paper (*optional*)

Procedure

Preparation Note: Distribute copies or display a large version of the poem "Sister's Bad Thursday" (page 94) and distribute *Hidden Th Words* (page 95) to students. Read the poem aloud or play the professional recording of the poem, and then proceed to the steps below.

1. Write the word *thump* on the board. Ask, "What word would I make if I change *th* to *b* in *thump*?" Erase the letters *th*, and write the letter *b*. Ask, "Were we right in our prediction about what the new word would be?"

2. Demonstrate this with other words such as *hump, lump,* and *dump.*

3. Write the word *thud* on the board. Say, "Look across the word and tell me all the sounds you hear." Or say, "Stretch the sounds as you read the word."

4. Repeat the activity with the word *thump.* Have students complete the activity page for additional practice.

#50974—Learning through Poetry: Consonant Blends and Digraphs

Content Connections

Social Studies

Materials

- "Sister's Bad Thursday" (page 94; Audio CD: Track 15)
- chart paper

Procedure

1. Reread the poem. Tell students that safety rules keep us from getting hurt. Ask students what rule Sister broke.

2. Ask students to give you some rules that keep us safe. Suggest that they think of safety rules at school. Why do we have each specific rule?

3. Suggest that students think of other rules, perhaps while in a car or walking to school. Make a list of students' responses and discuss why each rule was made to keep us safe.

Art

For an art activity supporting this lesson, please see the Digital Resource CD (artdigraphth.pdf).

School and Home Connection

Materials

- "Sister's Bad Thursday" (page 94)
- *Family Letter for Digraph Th* (page 96)
- chart with the following headings: *Student Name, Family Safety Rule, How It Keeps Us Safe*

Procedure

1. Attach the poem to the family letter.

2. When students return with their papers, ask them to share their families' rules. Write these on the chart.

3. Discuss what they learned.

Sister's Bad Thursday

By David L. Harrison

Sister tried to text and walk,
"Blah, blah, blah."

Thud!
She walked into a wall!

"Ha! Ha! Ha!"

"Don't laugh," she said,
"I hurt my thumb!"

"There, there, there."

She fussed at me
And didn't see the
Stair, stair, stair.

Sister thundered down the stairs,
Thump, thump, thump!
Bouncing on her derriere —
Rump, rump, rump!

Then she cried,
"My thigh feels broken!
Groan, groan, groan!"

Thursday's not my sister's day,
"Moan, moan, moan."

#50974—Learning through Poetry: Consonant Blends Band Digraphs

Name: _____ Date: _____

Hidden Th Words

Directions: Find and circle the *th* words below.

| the | thud | this | thump | that | those |

t	h	u	m	p	e	t	h	i	s
t	w	n	o	y	c	z	y	l	a
c	r	o	t	h	e	j	k	l	a
w	t	h	u	d	r	t	h	a	t
h	c	r	o	w	a	l	u	c	w
c	s	t	h	o	s	e	a	n	e

Use one of the words you found in a sentence.

_____

_____

_____

_____

#50974—Learning through Poetry: Consonant Blends and Digraphs

Dear Families,

This week, we read the poem "Sister's Bad Thursday." Enjoy reading it together with your student!

We have also been learning about safety rules. Ask your student what rules he or she heard about at school. Discuss with your student about a safety rule you have at home (such as not getting near the stove or standing on a chair to reach something). Discuss why your family has that rule and how it keeps the student safe. Share the rule you discussed with us by filling out the form below and returning it to school tomorrow.

Sincerely,

A safety rule our family has is:

_____

_____

_____

This is a rule because:

_____

_____

_____

#50974—Learning through Poetry: Consonant Blends and Digraphs   © Shell Education

Building Phonemic Awareness Skills

Materials

- "Whoop It Up!" (page 99; Audio CD: Track 16)
- chart paper (*optional*)

Procedure

Preparation Note: Distribute copies of the poem "Whoop It Up!" (page 99) to students or display a large version of the poem on chart paper. Read the poem aloud or play the professional recording of the poem, and then proceed to the steps below.

1. **Sound Matching**—Say to students, "Listen to these three words from the poem: *whistle, breeze, whisper*. Which have the same sounds at the beginning? Listen to these three words from the poem: *wheeze, boy, sneeze*. Which have the same sound at the end?"

2. **Sound Isolation**—Ask students, "What are the first sounds in the word *whimper*? What are the first sounds in the word *whirl*? In *whinny*?" Ask, "What other words begin with /wh/?"

3. **Sound Blending**—Ask students, "What word is /wh/ /ine/? What word is /wh/ /oosh/?"

4. **Sound Substitution**—Ask students, "What word would I make if I change /wh/ to /d/ in *whine*? If I change /wh/ to /g/ in *whirl*?"

5. **Sound Segmentation**—Ask students, "If you stretch the word *whiz*, what sounds do you hear? Stretch *whop*, what do you hear?"

Building Phonics Skills

Materials

- poem and activity page (pages 99–100)
- chart paper (*optional*)

Procedure

Preparation Note: Distribute copies or display a large version of the poem "Whoop It Up!" (page 99) and distribute *Making Pairs* (page 100) to students. Read the poem aloud or play the professional recording of the poem, and then proceed to the steps below.

1. Write the word *whine* on the board. Ask, "What word would I make if I change *wh* to *d* in *whine*?" Erase the letters *wh*, and write the letter *d*. Ask, "Were we right in our prediction about what the new word would be?"

2. Demonstrate this with other words such as *mine*, *fine*, and *nine*.

3. Write the word *whiz* on the board. Say, "Look across the word and tell me all the sounds you hear." Or say, "Stretch the sounds as you read the word."

4. Repeat the activity with the word *whoop*. Have students complete the activity page for additional practice.

....
Content Connections
....

Math

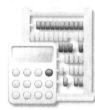

Materials

- "Whoop It Up!" (page 99; Audio CD: Track 16)
- items that come in pairs (e.g., socks, shoes, mittens, chopsticks)
- chart paper titled *Our Pairs*

Procedure

1. Show the poem to students, pointing out that the two voices are used to read. Pick two students to reread the poem with you.

2. Ask students if they know what we call sets of two (pairs). Give them a hint by asking what do they call two of the same shoe or two of the same socks.

3. Lay out the items you have that come in pairs, mixing them as you lay them out. Then ask students what they notice.

4. Model finding a pair (e.g., "Look, I see two of the same socks! That's a pair!").

5. Ask students to take turns finding a pair in the pile.

6. Ask students what pairs of things they have with them today. Record students' responses on the chart paper.

Art

For an art activity supporting this lesson, please see the Digital Resource CD (artdigraphwh.pdf).

School and Home Connection

Materials

- "Whoop It Up!" (page 99)
- *Family Letter for Digraph Wh* (page 101)
- chart paper with the following headings: *Student Name, Pair Found at Home*

Procedure

1. Attach the poem to the family letter.

2. When students return with their papers, ask them to share the pair they found at home. Record their answers on the chart.

4. Discuss what they learned—how many students found the same pair?

Whoop It Up!

By David L. Harrison

(1st voice)

Whistle like a teapot,

Whimper like a puppy dog,

Whinny like a race horse,

Whirl like a whirlybird,

Whop like a bellyflopper,

Whoosh on a dandelion,

(2nd voice)

Whoop like a boy,

Whir like a toy,

Whine like a brat,

Whiz like a bat,

Whisper like a breeze,

Wheeze and sneeze!

© Shell Education   #50974—Learning through Poetry: Consonant Blends and Digraphs

Name: _____ Date: _____

Making Pairs

Directions: Make pairs! Cut out the words below and glue the pairs of the same word in the boxes.

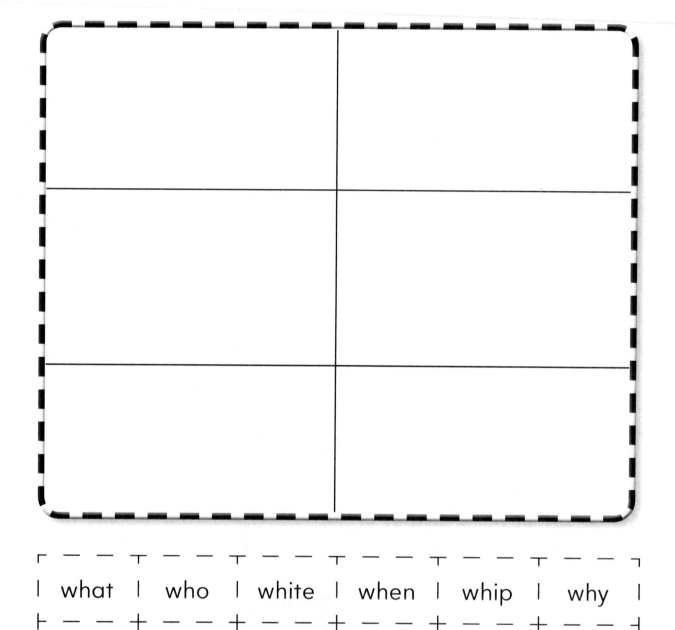

| what | who | white | when | whip | why |
| whip | why | when | white | what | who |

#50974—Learning through Poetry: Consonant Blends and Digraphs

Dear Families,

This week, we read the poem "Whoop It Up!" Enjoy reading it together with your student!

We have also been learning about pairs. We matched pairs of items during math time. We learned that a pair is two of something that match (socks, shoes). Please look around your home with your student and find pairs of items. Tell us below what you found and return this to school tomorrow.

Sincerely,

The pairs we found were:

_____

- -

_____

- -

_____

- -

_____

#50974—*Learning through Poetry: Consonant Blends and Digraphs*

References Cited

Adams, Marilyn J. 1990. *Beginning to Read: Thinking and Learning About Print*. Cambridge, MA: Massachusetts Institute of Technology Press.

Armbruster, Bonnie B., Fran Lehr, and Jean Osborn. 2001. *Put Reading First: The Research Building Blocks for Teaching Children to Read*. Washington, DC: National Institute for Literacy.

Dickmann, Nancy. 2010. *Food From Farms*. Chicago: Heinemann Chicago-Raintree.

Ehri, Linnea C., Simone R. Nunes, Dale M. Willows, Barbara Valeska Schuster, Zohreh Yaghoub-Zadeh, and Timothy Shanahan. 2001. "Phonemic Awareness Instruction Helps Children Learn to Read: Evidence from the National Reading Panel's Meta-analysis." *Reading Research Quarterly* 39(3): 250–287.

Ehri, Linnea C. and Theresa A. Roberts. 2006. "The Roots of Learning to Read and Write: Acquisition of Letters and Phonemic Awareness." In *Handbook of Early Literacy Research Volume 2*, edited by David K. Dickinson and Susan B. Neuman, 113–131. New York: Guilford Press.

Griffith, Priscilla L. and Mary W. Olson. 1992. "Phonemic Awareness Helps Beginning Readers Break the Code." In *The Reading Teacher* 45(7): 516–523.

Halliday, Michael A. K. 1975. *Learning How to Mean: Explorations in the Development of Language*. London: Edward Arnold.

Hart, Betty and Todd Risley. 2003. "The Early Catastrophe: The 30 Million Word Gap by Age 3." *American Educator* 27(1): 6–9.

Heilman, Arthur. 2002. *Phonics in Proper Perspective*, 9th ed. Columbus, OH: Merrill.

Inkelas, Sharon. 2003. "J's Rhymes: A Longitudinal Case Study of Language Play." *Journal of Child Language* 30(3): 557–581.

Juel, Connie. 2006. "The Impact of Early School Experiences on Initial Reading." In *Handbook of Early Literacy Research Volume 2*, edited by David K. Dickinson and Susan B. Neuman, 410–426. New York: Guilford.

Juel, Connie, Priscilla L. Griffith, and Philip B. Gough. 1986. "Acquisition of Literacy: A Longitudinal Study of Children in First and Second Grade." *Journal of Educational Psychology* 78(4): 243–255.

Lane, Holly B. and Paige C. Pullen. 2004. *Phonological Awareness Assessment and Instruction: A Sound Beginning*. Boston: Pearson.

References Cited (cont.)

National Early Literacy Panel. 2008. Developing Early Literacy: Report of the National Early Literacy Panel. Washington, DC: National Institute for Literacy.

National Institute of Child Health and Human Development. 2000. *Report of the National Reading Panel. Teaching Children to Read: An Evidence-Based Assessment of the Scientific Research Literature on Reading and Its Implications for Reading Instruction.* NIH Publication No. 00-4769. Washington, DC: U.S. Government Printing Office.

Opitz, Michael F. 2000. *Rhymes and Reasons: Literature and Language Play for Phonological Awareness.* Portsmouth, NH: Heinemann.

Padak, Nancy, and Terry Kindervater. 2008. "A 50-Year View of Family Literacy." In *An Essential History of Current Reading Practices*, edited by Mary Jo Fresch, 52–65. Newark, DE: International Reading Association.

Rasinski, Timothy V., and Nancy D. Padak. 2008. *From Phonics to Fluency: Effective Teaching of Decoding and Reading Fluency in the Elementary School.* 2nd ed. Boston: Pearson.

Rasinski, Timothy V., William H. Rupley, and William D. Nichols. 2008. "Two Essential Ingredients: Phonics and Fluency Getting to Know Each Other." *The Reading Teacher* 62 (3): 257–260.

Stahl, Steven A., and Bruce A. Murray. 1994. "Defining Phonological Awareness and its Relationship to Early Reading." In *Journal of Educational Psychology* 86(2): 221–234.

Stanovich, Keith E. 1993. "Romance and Reality." *The Reading Teacher* 47 (4): 280–291.

Trelease, Jim J. 1982. "Parade." *The Read-Aloud Handbook*, 18–19. New York: Penguin Books.

Walton, Patrick D., and Lona M. Walton. 2002. "Beginning Reading by Teaching in Rime Analogy: Effects on Phonological Skills, Letter-Sound Knowledge, Working Memory, and Word-Reading Strategies." In *Scientific Studies of Reading* 6 (1): 79–115.

Wasik, Barbara A. 2010. "What Teachers Can Do to Promote Preschoolers' Vocabulary Development: Strategies for Effective Language and Literacy Professional Development Coaching Model." *Reading Teacher* 63 (8): 621–633.

Wylie, Richard E., and Donald D. Durrell. 1970. "Teaching Vowels Through Phonograms. In *Elementary School Journal* 47(6): 787–791.

Wylie, Richard E., and Donald D. Durrell. 1970. "Teaching Vowels Through Phonograms. In *Elementary School Journal* 47(6): 787–791.

Answer Key

Bl or B? (page 25)

The following words should start with *bl*: *block, blouse, blanket.*

The following words should start with *b*: *bird, boat, bone.*

Match the Picture (page 30)

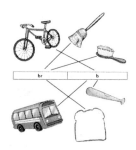

Complete the Words (page 35)

The following words begin *cl*: *clean, clap, clay, clip.*

Students' sentences will vary but should include one of the *cl* words.

CRossword Fun (page 40)

c	r	i	c	k	e	t
e	c	r	a	z	y	r
c	r	o	c	y	o	w
w	c	r	e	a	m	e
h	c	r	o	w	a	m
c	s	c	r	a	n	e

Students' sentences will vary but should include one of the *cr* words.

Making Fl Words (page 45)

Students should write the following *fl* words: *flea, flew, fly, flag, flip, flat*

Students' sentences will vary but should include one of the *fl* words.

Matching F Words (page 50)

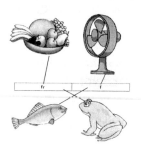

GReat Words (page 55)

The following words begin with *gr*: *grin, gruff, groan, grill, grand, grab.*

Students' sentences will vary but should include one of the *gr* words.

Pl Crossword (page 60)

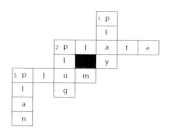

Perfect Fit (page 65)

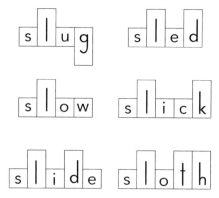

#50974—*Learning through Poetry: Consonant Blends and Digraphs*   © Shell Education

Sorting Sn Words (page 70)

The following words begin with *sn*: *snowflake, snake, snail, snowman*

The following words begin with *s*: *sun, spoon, star, spider*

Sp Words (page 75)

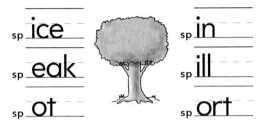

sp **ice**

sp **eak**

sp **ot**

sp **in**

sp **ill**

sp **ort**

Students' sentences will vary but should use one of the *sp* words.

Circling St Words (page 80)

Students should circle the following pictures: *strawberry, stomach, stick, star*.

Is It Ch or C? (page 85)

Students should circle the following: c for carrot, ch for chicken, ch for chin, ch for chair, ch for cheese, c for car.

Time to Sort! (page 90)

The following words begin with *Sh*: *shank, shark, sheep, ship, shirt, shun*.

The following words begin with *S*: *sand, seep sip, sank, sun, save, saw*.

Hidden Th Words (page 95)

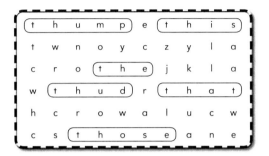

Students' sentences will vary but should include one of the *th* words.

Making Pairs (page 100)

what	what	who	who
whip	whip	why	why
when	when	white	white

Content Connection Matrix

The following chart notes the content area and art lessons possible with each poem.

Poem	Content Area	Arts Connection	Pages
"Black and Blue"	Science—Bird watching	Bird mobile	22–26
"Bratty"	Social Studies—Rules	Charades	27–31
"Clara"	Social Studies—Similar and different likes	Wind instruments	32–36
"Croc and Cricket"	Math—Comparing sizes	Paper mosaics	37–41
"Fly and Flea"	Science—Flight	Butterflies in flight	42–46
"Fraidy Cat Frank"	Science—Frog life cycle	Imitate a Ffog	47–51
"Grandmas"	Math—Cooking	Paper bag bears	52–56
"Plink"	Science—Sink and float	Float or sink pictures	57–61
"Slippery"	Science—Weather	Snow pictures	62–66
"Snack"	Math—Measurement	Bookmark	67–71
"Spunky Sparrow"	Social Studies—Food from around the world	Painting flags	72–76
"When Kings Meet"	Social Studies—Families nighttime routines	Watercolor sunset	77–81
"Choosy"	Science—Healthy ating; Dairy group	Torn paper cheesy food	82–86
"Shirley the Shark"	Social Studies—Trip to the ocean	Sand art	87–91
"Sister's Bad Thursday"	Social Studies—Safety rules	Safety posters	92–96
"Whoop It Up!"	Math—Pairs	Sock pairs that match	97–101

#50974—*Learning through Poetry: Consonant Blends and Digraphs*

Contents of the CDs

Contents of the Digital Resource CD

Poems		
Page	**Title**	**Filename**
24	"Black and Blue"	blackblue.pdf
29	"Bratty"	bratty.pdf
34	"Clara"	clara.pdf
39	"Croc and Cricket"	croccricket.pdf
44	"Fly and Flea"	flyflea.pdf
49	"Fraidy Cat Frank"	fraidycat.pdf
54	"Grandmas"	grandmas.pdf
59	"Plink"	plink.pdf
64	"Slippery"	slippery.pdf
69	"Snack"	snack.pdf
74	"Spunky Sparrow"	sparrow.pdf
79	"When Kings Meet"	kingsmeet.pdf
84	"Choosy"	choosy.pdf
89	"Shirley the Shark"	shirleyshark.pdf
94	"Sister's Bad Thursday"	sisterthursday.pdf
99	"Whoop It Up!"	whoopitup.pdf

Activity Pages		
Page	**Title**	**Filename**
25	Bl or B?	blorb.pdf
30	Match the Picture	matchpicture.pdf
35	Complete the Words	completewords.pdf
40	CRossword Fun	crosswordfun.pdf
45	Making Fl Words	flwords.pdf
50	Matching F Words	matchingf.pdf
55	GReat Words	greatwords.pdf
60	Pl Crossword	plcrossword.pdf
65	Perfect Fit	perfectfit.pdf
70	Sorting Sn Words	sortingsnwords.pdf
75	Sp Words	spwords.pdf
80	Circling St Words	stwords.pdf
85	Is It Ch or C?	isitchorc.pdf
90	Time to Sort!	timetosort.pdf
95	Hidden Th Words	hiddenthwords.pdf
100	Making Pairs	makingpairs.pdf

Correlation Charts	
CCSS, WIDA, TESOL, and McREL	standards.pdf

#50974—*Learning through Poetry: Consonant Blends and Digraphs*

Contents of the Digital Resource CD (cont.)

Art Activity Pages	
Title	**Filename**
Blend Bl	artblendbl.pdf fieldguide.pdf birdoutline.pdf
Blend Br	artblendbr.pdf
Blend Cl	artblendcl.pdf
Blend Cr	artblendcr.pdf
Blend Fl	artblendfl.pdf
Blend Fr	artblendfr.pdf lilypad.pdf frogfeet.pdf
Blend Gr	artblendgr.pdf
Blend Pl	artblendpl.pdf
Blend Sl	artblendsl.pdf
Blend Sn	artblendsn.pdf snailandsnake.pdf
Blend Sp	artblendsp.pdf
Blend St	artblendst.pdf horse.pdf
Digraph Ch	artdigraphch.pdf
Digraph Sh	artdigraphsh.pdf
Digraph Th	artdigraphth.pdf
Digraph Wh	artdigraphwh.pdf

Family Letters		
Page	**Title**	**Filename**
26	Family Letter for Blend Bl	letterblendbl.pdf letterblendbl.doc
31	Family Letter for Blend Br	letterblendbr.pdf letterblendbr.doc
36	Family Letter for Blend Cl	letterblendcl.pdf letterblendcl.doc
41	Family Letter for Blend Cr	letterblendcr.pdf letterblendcr.doc
46	Family Letter for Blend Fl	letterblendfl.pdf letterblendfl.doc
51	Family Letter for Blend Fr	letterblendfr.pdf letterblendfr.doc
56	Family Letter for Blend Gr	letterblendgr.pdf letterblendgr.doc
61	Family Letter for Blend Pl	letterblendpl.pdf letterblendpl.doc
66	Family Letter for Blend Sl	letterblendsl.pdf letterblendsl.doc
71	Family Letter for Blend Sn	letterblendsn.pdf letterblendsn.doc
76	Family Letter for Blend Sp	letterblendsp.pdf letterblendsp.doc
81	Family Letter for Blend St	letterblendst.pdf letterblendst.doc
86	Family Letter for Digraph Ch	letterdigraphch.pdf letterdigraphch.doc
91	Family Letter for Digraph Sh	letterdigraphsh.pdf letterdigraphsh.doc
96	Family Letter for Digraph Th	letterdigraphth.pdf letterdigraphth.doc
101	Family Letter for Digraph Wh	letterdigraphwh.pdf letterdigraphwh.doc

Contents of the CDs *(cont.)*

Contents of the Audio CD

Meet the Authors

David Harrison, Litt. D, is a nationally acclaimed author and poet. He has written more than seventy-five books of poetry, fiction, and nonfiction for young readers and has been anthologized in countless others. His work has been translated into twelve languages and has been aired on television, radio, podcast, and video stream. David has authored many professional and classroom resources for teachers, including *Partner Poems for Building Fluency: 40 Engaging Poems for Two Voices with Motivating Activities That Help Students Improve Their Fluency and Comprehension* with Timothy Rasinski and Gay Fawcett. He has even created a video series, *Let's Write This Week with David Harrison*, that brings writing tips into the elementary classroom and offers graduate college credit for teachers. David holds degrees from Drury University and Emory University and holds honorary doctorates of letters from Missouri State University and Drury University where he is the current poet laureate. David Harrison Elementary School is named in his honor.

- -

To Nancy Raider, for patiently answering all my questions about 5th graders.

With special thanks to my friend and writing partner, Mary Jo Fresch, for making these books such a fun journey.

— DLH

Mary Jo Fresch, Ph.D., is a professor at The Ohio State University at Marion, Department of Teaching and Learning. She holds a bachelor of science in elementary education, a master of science in Reading Supervision/Specialist, and a doctor of philosophy in Language, Literacy, and Culture. She has taught elementary school, adult literacy, and literacy methods courses. She has also taught at the University of Akron and the University of Nebraska—Lincoln, and internationally at the Royal Melbourne Institute of Technology and Deakin University. Her research focuses on the developmental aspects of becoming a speller and its relationship to teaching and learning. Her articles have appeared in *The Reading Teacher, Reading Online, Language Arts, Journal of Literacy Research, Reading and Writing Quarterly, Reading Psychology,* and several state literacy journals. Mary Jo's natonal and international presentations focus on literacy learning and English orthography.

- -

To my children and their spouses, Angela and Nate... Mike and Lori—for showing my grandsons how to love.

With special thanks to my friend and writing partner, David Harrison, who paints the world with beautiful words.

— MJF

#50974—Learning through Poetry: Consonant Blends and Digraphs   © Shell Education

Notes

 #50974—Learning through Poetry: Consonant Blends and Digraphs

Notes

#50974—*Learning through Poetry: Consonant Blends and Digraphs*   © Shell Education